T0305886

Data Analytics in Project Management

Data Analytics Applications

Series Editor:
Jay Liebowitz

For more information about this series, please visit: https://www.crcpress.com/Data-Analytics-Applications/book-series/CRCDATANAAPP

Data Analytics in Project Management

Edited by
Seweryn Spalek

CRC Press
Taylor & Francis Group
Boca Raton London New York

CRC Press is an imprint of the
Taylor & Francis Group, an **informa** business

CRC Press
Taylor & Francis Group
6000 Broken Sound Parkway NW, Suite 300
Boca Raton, FL 33487-2742

First issued in paperback 2021

ISBN-13: 978-1-138-30728-5 (hbk)

ISBN-13: 978-1-03-209452-6 (pbk)

Library of Congress Cataloging-in-Publication Data

Names: Spalek, Seweryn, editor.
Title: Data analytics in project management / edited by Seweryn Spalek.
Description: Boca Raton, FL : CRC Press, [2019] | Includes bibliographical references and index.
Identifiers: LCCN 2018029001 | ISBN 9781138307285 (alk. paper) | ISBN 9780429434891 (alk. paper)
Subjects: LCSH: Project management—Data processing. | Project management—Statistical methods.
Classification: LCC HD69.P75 D374 2019 | DDC 658.4/040285—dc23
LC record available at https://lccn.loc.gov/2018029001

**Visit the Taylor & Francis Web site at
http://www.taylorandfrancis.com**

**and the CRC Press Web site at
http://www.crcpress.com**

Contents

About the Editor

Seweryn Spalek, PhD, MSc, ICT-Eng., is a Professor of Business and Management at Silesian University of Technology, Poland. He possesses extensive knowledge and expertise in project management, both in theory and practice. Since 1994, he has managed several IT projects in industrial companies and healthcare organizations in multicultural and multinational environments and has managed an organizational change project—redesigning the functional organization to project-oriented organization with PMO; has established and has been running portfolio management of over 500 projects per year within organization. Spalek is the author and co-author of several publications in project management and is the author of *The Art of War in Project Management*. He has participated as a speaker in several global conferences related to project management and company management. Spalek is a lecturer of MBA and post graduate studies and company management focusing on applied project management. He has carried out research related to key success factors in project management and project management maturity. Spalek is a member of AOM (Academy of Management), PMI (Project Management Institute), and IPMA (International Project Management Association), and the Director-at-Large at SEFI (La Société Européenne pour la Formation des Ingénieurs/The European Society for Engineering Education).

Contributors

Michael Bragen is an expert in the governance and management of people, processes, and technologies that support, leverage, and enhance innovation. His work focuses on the use of data and analytics supporting project and portfolio management, estimation, and process improvement. As a strategic advisor to large organizations around the world, Bragen has conducted hundreds of performance assessments and established analytics practices for clients. Bragen is the director of global marketing and partner development at Computer Aid, Inc. (http://www.compaid.com), an IT services firm headquartered in Allentown, Pennsylvania.

Bert Brijs is a practitioner in business analysis, project management, and architectures in analytics and customer relationship management. He bundled his 30+ years of European, Asian, and American experience in the book *Business Analysis for Business Intelligence*, which combines practical tips and tricks with academic insights. A fluent speaker of six languages, Brijs bridges gaps between different cultures, an extension of his work as an analyst where he bridges the gap between business and IT.

Alfonso Bucero, MSc, PMP, PMI-RMP, PfMP, PMI Fellow, and Certified Public Speaker, is an independent project management consultant, author, and speaker. He is founder, partner, and director of BUCERO PM Consulting in Spain. Bucero has an M.S. in computer science engineering. He is the author of nine project management books and manages projects internationally. He delivers workshops, keynote speeches, and consults organizations on project program and portfolio management. His motto is passion, persistence, and patience and for him every day is a good day. ("Today is a good day" is his preferred sentence.)

Yanping Chen, PhD, MD, PMP, PMI Fellow, has been running major education and training programs in China and the United States since the mid-1980s. Prior to coming to the United States in 1987, she was the planning director for China's manned space flight program, where 200 projects were being carried out concurrently. She has taught at the

George Washington University and the International Space University. Her areas of expertise include international business management, project management, public administration, public policy, science and technology policy and management, entrepreneurship, and leadership. During 1992–1995, Dr. Chen served on the Certification Committee of the Project Management Institute (PMI). She was elected to PMI's Board of Directors from 2005–2010. In 2008, she was elected to serve as vice chair of the Project Management Institute. In 2012, she was made a Fellow of the PMI. Dr. Chen has authored more than 20 publications covering a broad range of international science and technology policy and management issues as well as medical technical issues. She is author of the book *Principles of Contracting for Project Management.*

J. Davidson Frame, PhD, PMP, PMI Fellow, is an academic dean at the University of Management and Technology (UMT), Arlington, Virginia. He has been active in project management theory and practice for more than 30 years. He has written eight project management books, two of which were business best sellers: *Managing Projects in Organizations* and *The New Project Management.* Prior to joining UMT, he spent 19 years on the faculty of George Washington (GW) University, where he established GW's graduate degree program in project management. At GW, he served as chair of the management science department and director of the Program on Science, Technology, and Innovation. As a consultant and educator, Dr. Frame has worked with a wide range of organizations, including some 40 federal, state, and municipal agencies as well as many major corporations, including AT&T, Motorola, Hewlett-Packard, Morgan Stanley, Credit Suisse, IBM, Nokia, ABB, Compaq, Sprint, Freddie Mac, and Fannie Mae. He has been active in the Project Management Institute (PMI) since the 1990s and in 2004 was named a Fellow of the institute.

Deanne Larson, MBA, MSBA, DM, PhD, is an active data mining practitioner and academician. Her doctoral dissertation research focused on a grounded theory qualitative study on establishing enterprise data strategy. Her second dissertation researched communication factors in data science and analytics projects. She holds Project Management Professional (PMP), Certified Business Intelligence Profession (CBIP), and Six Sigma certifications. Larson attended AT&T executive training at the Harvard

Business School, focusing on IT leadership, Stanford University, focusing on data mining, and New York University, focusing on business analytics. She presents several times a year at conferences for The Data Warehouse Institute (TDWI). Dr. Larson is the principal faculty at City University of Seattle and has consulted for several Fortune 500 companies.

Ryan Legard specializes in quantitative program management, where he uses quantitative tools and their data to inform better program management decision-making. He is a lead associate in Booz Allen Hamilton's Strategic Innovation Group, where he supports a variety of customers in the public and private sectors. Prior to joining Booz Allen, he provided program management and analysis support to several Fortune 500 companies in the defense, aerospace, and IT markets.

Ryan holds a bachelor of arts degree in political science from the University of Central Florida, a master of arts degree in political science from George Mason University, and a project management professional (PMP) certification from the Project Management Institute. His interests in project management include the integration of cost, schedule, and risk variables to enable probabilistic and predictive analytics.

Werner Meyer, PhD, is a director at ProjectLink Consulting, a project management consulting and training company in South Africa. He obtained his PhD in strategy, program, and portfolio management from SKEMA Business School France, and has more than 20 years of experience in project, program, and portfolio management. He is responsible for research and development at ProjectLink, and his current research interests include decision-making, neuroeconomics, quantitative risk analysis, and machine learning. He also holds a position as extraordinary senior lecturer at the University of Pretoria.

Carl Pritchard, PMP, PMI-RMP, is the principal and founder of Pritchard Management Associates, a training firm based in Frederick, Maryland. He is the author of seven texts in project management, and serves as the U.S. correspondent for the UK project management magazine, *Project Manager Today.* He teaches risk, project management, and communications around the globe. He welcomes your thoughts and insights at carl@carlpritchard.com.

Klas Skogmar, PMP, EMBA, is a management consultant with an extensive background in project, program, and portfolio management. Klas has been part of ISO standardization of project portfolio management, governance, and WBS, and regularly holds courses and seminars in areas such as PMBOK, ISO, PRINCE2, and agile development. He is also an entrepreneur with experience from founding and managing companies in various industries over the years. As a methodology specialist, he has helped large organizations such as IKEA, Ikano, Sony Mobile, Gambro, Tetra Pak, Alfa Laval, and the Swedish Social Insurance Agency with portfolio management, project management, and organizational agility.

1

Introduction

Seweryn Spalek

Data analytics (DA) plays a crucial role in business analytics. Without a rigid approach to analyzing data, we wouldn't be able to glean insights from it. According to Evan Stubbs,[*] strong analytical abilities are a prerequisite to taking action and creating change, which then must be followed by identification, communication, delivery, and measurement of the value of business analytics. Furthermore, data is usually produced in massive amounts nowadays, and that tendency will continue to increase dramatically. This data production on a massive scale also happens with the Internet of Things (IoT), and, as we near the fourth industrial revolution, the number of sources of data is soaring. Machines connected through the Cloud will create large amounts of data associated with their daily tasks. Moreover, the IoT, interacting with humans, will add additional sets of information. A digital transformation without numerous flows of data would be impossible. This means that projects will be surrounded by or even immersed in oceans of data. Therefore, we need, more urgently than ever, to have mechanisms in place that are able to acquire this data, and then clean, aggregate, and present it. This process is often called the management of data. Then analytics comes in with models and analysis, moving toward a final interpretation. Hence, DA is an extremely important and central part of the entire process. It should, in short, be seen as a driver leading to change, as shown in Figure 1.1.

Business analytics ensures the expected value of change, while that change is implemented by projects in the business environment. With the significant increase in the number of projects and the amount of data associated with them, it is crucial to understand the areas in which DA can be applied in project management (PM). Therefore, in this book, we address DA in relation to key areas, approaches, and methods in PM.

---

[*] The value of business analytics, in: *Business Analytics. An Introduction.* Jay Liebowitz (ed.), CRC Press, Taylor & Francis Group, Boca Raton, FL.

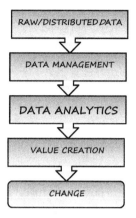

FIGURE 1.1
The key role of data analytics in the process of driving change in project management.

Thus, in Chapter 2, J. Davidson Frame and Yanping Chen, in an excellent way, address the question: Why data analytics in project management? They note the differences between ancient and modern data analyses. Then they show the evolutionary path from Analytics 1.0 to Analytics 2.0 and reveal that it is necessary for PM DA to combine two inputs coming from business analytics and PM metrics. This means not only relying on historical, real-time, and prescriptive data, but also on strategic key performance indicators (KPIs), financials, marketing, operations, supply chains, and external factors. Moreover, this means depending on planning and controlling the data concerning schedules, budgets, specs, resources, and work performance. The authors address the importance of the data warehouse in the entire analytical process and outline its configuration. Moreover, they present the value that project DA brings to the key players: project manager, project office, chief operating officer, and the executive committee. Frame and Chen include relevant examples and business cases to better explain their reasoning, especially when describing descriptive, predictive, and prescriptive DA. At the end of the chapter, the authors outline the vision (or near future?) of Analytics 3.0, including the key aspects of real time, the tracking of trillions of data points, artificial intelligence, and machine learning.

Risk is associated with any type of activity while managing projects. We can ignore risk, but it will not ignore us. Therefore, Carl Pritchard, in Chapter 3, addresses this important topic in relation to DA in PM. He describes the tolerance issue and its implications. Moreover, he outlines the qualitative approach to data, asking the question: How big is big? He also examines the main sources of bias in data flows. Thus, he discusses the issues associated with data sourcing and its consistency. Further, he explains the concepts of exploratory, confirmatory, and predictive risks in DA. Finally, Pritchard discusses the very important topic of communicating results and the risks associated with them. He points out that the timing of the former is crucial, as well as the means of communication, and underlines that communication, if done improperly, can even be harmful. All of this is explored in an engaging narrative style, aided by a plethora of excellent cases.

The amount of data associated with projects is enormous nowadays and will likely soar. Therefore, there is a need to somehow systematize company data flows, and it appears that the project management office (PMO) is best positioned to oversee this process. This idea is described in Chapter 4. To cope with new challenges, PMOs need to evolve from their current stages toward analytical maturity in the areas of methods and tools, human resources, project environments, and project knowledge management. As data can be obtained from different sources, the concept of the PMO as a multilevel data analysis center is presented. Moreover, the crucial issue of delivering data to the project, portfolio, and organization outcome levels is discussed. As each project interacts with the operations, tactics, and strategies of a company, that issue is outlined, as well. Finally, the concept of the PMO as the centralized office for data flows in a multi-dimensional project and company environment is proposed.

Projects nowadays are no longer treated by organizations as single, separate endeavors. Companies group them together in portfolios according to the value they should bring to the organization. This creates additional sets of data, which should be analyzed properly. Therefore, Alfonso Bucero focuses on applying DA in project portfolio management (PPM) in a lively and engaging manner. He argues that the focus should be on four dimensions for portfolio optimization: cost value, resources, schedules, and work type. To make this a reality, he proposes the application of a five-step methodology, consisting of the following stages: define, adapt, visualize, assess, and recommend. Furthermore, he explains why DA is key for the decision-making process in PPM and how it can cooperate with business performance management (BPM). Finally, he outlines the issue of DA and project portfolio performance.

When discussing DA, the earned value method (EVM) definitely should be mentioned since EVM is widely recognized and used in PM. This topic is covered by Werner Meyer in Chapter 6. Using a very good and clear approach, he explains such terms as budget at completion, planned value, actual cost, and, finally, earned value. All of these terms belong to descriptive EVM, while predictive EVM covers estimate at completion, estimate to complete, variance at completion, to complete performance index, and time estimate at completion indicators. Furthermore, the interpretation of EVM results is explained. Finally, Werner Meyer highlights the pitfalls of using EVM.

The concept of "big data" occurs in more and more situations these days. Therefore, it is crucial to discuss this concept in the context of PM. Thus, in Chapter 7, Ryan Legard at first explains what attributes differentiate big data from other types of data. Demonstrating his mastery of the subject he discusses, on a step-by-step basis, how to handle big data in projects. In doing so, he distinguishes between three general types or categories of data: structured, unstructured, and semistructured. He proposes a scheme for pairing data with analytical methods taking into account storage technologies. Moreover, he provides advice on how to establish proper controls in order to use the effects of big data analysis as success enablers. He covers important topics such as the means with which to communicate value statements and the chief data officer, a new job title across many organizations. Furthermore, Ryan Legard elaborates on biases in data collection, noting that they are most common during the early stages of organizational and data analysis maturity. Finally, he proposes resolutions for common big data issues.

Managing data cannot be done without information technology (IT) support, which is currently present in many aspects of a company's activities. Therefore, Michael Bragen competently guides the reader through the main ideas and outlines the key characteristics which type of software should have to support DA in Chapter 8. He underlines the need for functionality in terms of early warning signs and associated metrics. Then, based on an example of an online system used for visibility and control, he presents different dashboard scenarios. He also discusses an enterprise governance system based on an interesting case study. As it is crucial that each IT system is located within a company, he presents a list of implementation challenges and how to deal with them. Finally, he outlines the future of automated analytical tools, geared toward artificial intelligence operations technology.

Managing projects means making decisions. This process can be supported by data mining, which is the selection, refinement, and analysis of data in order to make decisions or resolve some type of problem. Klas Skogmar, in Chapter 9, capably tackles the key issues via cogent analyses and clear understanding on this important topic by, first, explaining the difference between "doing the right thing" and "doing things right." Then, he discusses the five aspects of bad decisions, which are biases, bad data, wrong data, too much data, and not using the data. Among these many important aspects, he explains the "bias bias" phenomenon. Moreover, he discusses how to make good decisions and provides three steps with which to improve the way decisions are made. Next, Skogmar explains how to conduct data mining in four steps, starting with the collection of data, then moving on to mining the information, regression analysis, and, finally, presenting and concluding. Furthermore, he discusses how to extend beyond traditional data mining techniques to improve project success rates. His point is that, in order to do so, unconventional methods should be utilized. He proposes using (1) the lean startup best practice framework or (2) reinforcing or steering behavior. Finally, he explores the possibility of using machine learning methods, or artificial intelligence, to aid in decision-making.

In today's turbulent environment, an increasing number of projects are run using the agile approach. Although developed for IT, this approach is being adapted by other industries with progressive success. Thus, Deanne Larson, in Chapter 10, shows her prowess by skillfully addressing, in a straightforward fashion, the important issues of agile PM and DA. At first, she describes the change in the data landscape that has occurred over time, focusing on three data characteristics: volume, variety, then velocity and veracity. Moreover, noting that existing approaches need to be more dynamic, she discusses the methods used in DA projects. Then, she goes into detail concerning agile software development (ASD) principles and CRISP-DM, a data mining process model that describes conceptually the stages that are used to tackle data mining problems. She goes on to discuss the alignment of ASD values and CRISP-DM, as well as the challenges of ASD as applied to DA. Next, she describes best practices in DA PM, starting with the importance of due diligence in defining business goals and problem statements. Further, she examines the issue of underestimating the time required to acquire data for a project and the technical tools that are needed for analytical modeling and data wrangling. Finally, Larson spells out future trends and efforts in the agile approach and DA.

Since Scrum is currently the most popular agile software development method, Brijs Bert sensibly takes a practical approach in Chapter 11 to the issue and goes into this method in some detail. Being aware of the challenging nature of his chapter, he likens combining DA and Scrum as something akin to mixing oil and water together. However, what, at first, seems to be an insurmountable task proves to be well within his grasp. He begins by explaining online transactional processing (OLTP) and online analytical processing (OLAP). He then describes the contrasts between OLAP and OLTP with respect to DA. In addition, he discusses the type of business intelligence (BI) project that may provide a project manager with analytical support. Finally, based on his considerations, he proposes the use of the Sprint Minus One approach in setting up an analytical model, just as a Sprint Zero approach is used for setting up the technical environment.

DA in PM is of increasing importance but extremely challenging. On the one hand, there is rapid multiplication of data volumes, and, on the other hand, the structure of the data is more and more complex. Digging through exabytes of data currently and zettabytes in the close future is a technological challenge in and of itself. When the basic needs of PM to create value are placed on top of that, we face a real concern. In this book, we try to address the most common issues of applying DA in PM. Through supporting theory with numerous examples and case studies, we would like this book to be both valuable for academics and practitioners alike. Although we are aware that the topic of DA in PM is much wider than the topics presented in this book, we hope that we will at least shed some light on the topic by discussing the current state of applications of DA in PM and future developments.

2

Why Data Analytics in Project Management?

J. Davidson Frame and Yanping Chen

CONTENTS

Broadly speaking, data analytics entails the systematic use of data to guide decision-making in organizations. It requires acquiring pertinent data, organizing it, discerning meaningful patterns in it, and determining how the newly gained insights can guide decision-making. By following this process, decision makers minimize reliance on guesswork and gut feeling and engage in evidence-based decision-making.

This chapter addresses the question, why data analytics in project management?

In a broad sense, data analytics is not new to project management. Consider the Giza pyramid, which was built 4,500 years ago. Given the enormity of the construction effort and the astonishing logistical challenges of quarrying, cutting, shipping, and emplacing some 2.3 million stone blocks, each weighing 2.5 to 15 tons, it is clear that the pyramid builders engaged in some sort of analysis that entailed a review of historical data coupled with making estimates of material and logistical requirements for the new structure. Since the time of the Giza pyramid through the nineteenth century, many major construction projects have been carried out, each of which required sorting through data and using the information gleaned from it to plan and implement the work effort. Some of the information was historical, which reflected learning from past project experiences, good or bad, and some new efforts, capturing the unique requirements of the current project.

What is new since the mid-twentieth century is the conscious collection, documentation, and employment of data for the purpose of executing projects effectively. Until fairly recently, data-driven learning was captured in the heads of the players through apprenticeship. On a large project, a highly experienced master-builder would play the role of a project manager, and a collection of various workers would serve under him. They learned their trade on the job, and as they assumed senior roles themselves, they would pass their learning on to the next generation of apprentices.

This chapter examines the evolution of data analytics employed in projects, from the 1950s through today. Following Davenport (2013), it notes that data analytics has gone through two major stages: before big data (1950s through mid-2000s, which we term Analytics 1.0) and after big data (mid-2000s through today, which we call Analytics 2.0). With Analytics 1.0, decision makers employed whatever data that was available to inform their decision-making. At the outset, the data focused on internal operations. What materials were available to produce something? How long did the production effort take? What did it cost? Analysis of the data was chiefly directed at employing it to improve the operations of the enterprise. Data collection and analysis were largely serendipitous with little consideration for collecting and integrating metrics across the full range of the business of the enterprise. The data used was the data that happened to be captured. On occasions when business entities used data to improve the management of their operations, their findings were constrained by the data that was available. Still, even in this primitive situation, the decisions that were made informed by data. In a sense, it could be assumed that data analytics has been employed in project management since the time of the pyramids.

Analytics 2.0 is built on the foundation established by Analytics 1.0, but it incorporates a major shift in perspective. For example, while Analytics 1.0 is focused heavily on structuring data associated with an organization's operations so that it can be analyzed, Analytics 2.0 handles nonstructured data (noSQL), accommodates audio and visual information and incorporates data from outside the organization, as well as from all parts of the business.

Furthermore, as the big data appellation suggests, it works with very large data sets. Algorithms used to analyze small data are often inefficient when applied to big data. Today, the data we process is not just quantitatively different from what we handled a decade ago, but qualitatively different as well. The 3Vs describe the three aspects of super big data that distinguish it from what was previously viewed as large data sets in the recent past (Stapleton, 2011). The 3Vs address data volume, velocity, and variety.

- *Data volume.* Big data today may entail handling petabytes (1,024 terabytes) or even exabytes (1,024 petabytes) of data, comprising billions or trillions of records of millions of people.
- *Data velocity.* To be usable, the astonishingly large volumes of data need to be handled at breakneck speed. All elements of data management—collecting, processing, and using large amounts of data—must be carried out in nanoseconds or faster. Methods of working with high volumes of data at high speed are required to employ radical rethinking of how data can be processed. For example, with Analytics 1.0, raw data is stored in column and row format, which is analyzed with conventional tools. Today, to gain usable insights from super large data sets (including unstructured data), the data is transformed and analyzed as it arrives. If it reveals a certain pattern, it is then flagged and analyzed for further high-speed in-depth review.
- *Data variety.* Analytics 1.0 is carried out using traditional business metrics covering basic operations. With Analytics 2.0, attention is focused on processing different categories of data, including numerical, audio, video, image, text messages, traditional text, and social media data (e.g., tweets), much of it unstructured.

When using the term "project data analytics," it is important to take stock of which stage is being addressed. Leading edge Analytics 2.0 today can include machine learning and artificial intelligence in addition to a host of advanced statistical and operations research techniques. Its best-known practitioners include information technology giants like Amazon, Google, and Facebook. It incorporates insights from psychology, linguistics, the market behavior of individuals, logistics, and the supply chain, as well as an understanding of what actions competitors are taking now and are likely to take in the future, and wedding the totality of this and other knowledge to the full range of capabilities of the organization. Its most obvious employment is on large, complex projects. Large construction projects and defense projects integrate data on procurement, the supply chain, and the project work effort. Aircraft design-and-build projects carried out by Boeing and Airbus make heavy use of data analytics to accommodate these factors on a global scale, taking into account the production and assembly of different components of aircraft in different countries, and also considering external factors such as different trade regulations across the globe. Project Analytics 1.0, in contrast, typically restricts its attention to an enterprise's basic data on cost, schedule, quality, and requirements, with a view to using this data to understand and improve project and operational performance.

TAKING ROOT

The conscious and systematic use of data to inform managerial decisions is rooted in the work of the American industrial engineer, Frederick Winslow Taylor, whose studies in the late nineteenth and early twentieth centuries laid the foundation for "scientific management." He focused on using empirical data to identify more effective ways to carry out work efforts. His insights had a significant impact on manufacturing enterprises, consultants, and academics and triggered a new profession that comprised efficiency experts. However, it was not until the 1950s that what we currently view as bona fide data analytics took root in organizations. At this time, the introduction of computers into business and government organizations made possible the collection and storage of large quantities of data covering all aspects of the operations of the organization, including production, payroll, purchasing, human resources (HR), administration, and more. It quickly became apparent that this data could be used to improve businesses processes.

Coincidentally, the conscious employment of project-related data to manage projects effectively also arose at this time. In 1957, the program evaluation and review technique (PERT) was developed by the US Navy in order to schedule the building of submarines in the Polaris Missile Program, and in 1958 the critical path method (CPM) was developed at DuPont. By creating system flow charts that portrayed the interrelationships among activities and events, both techniques enabled project engineers to develop detailed project schedules on large, complex projects. PERT and CPM models could also be used to provide guidance on how to accelerate schedules cost effectively.

Additional project management methodology innovations that had a bearing on project data analytics arose at this time. The development of configuration management in the 1950s and earned value management in the late 1960s dramatically demonstrated the value of employing systems thinking coupled with cost, schedule, and requirements metrics to manage large, complex programs effectively. Because these techniques required the computing power of mainframe computers, they were initially inaccessible to small and medium-sized projects. That changed in 1982 with the advent of Harvard Project Manager, a colorful and engaging software package that made the sophisticated techniques of integrated cost and schedule planning and control accessible to the smallest projects at an affordable price ($265). With the arrival of affordable, friendly, PC-based project scheduling and budgeting packages, project data analytics gained a toe-hold in small and medium-sized organizations.

THE VIEW FROM 10,000 METERS

Figure 2.1 offers a mind map that highlights the constituent components of project data analytics. It portrays how conventional business data analytics and project performance metrics come together to constitute project data analytics. It shows how project data analytics goes beyond concern for the standard project metrics that have formed the basis of analyzing project performance since the 1950s, with their focus on schedules, budgets, resource allocations, specifications, and work performance assessments, and accommodates business and environmental factors as well.

It incorporates the full range of Analytics 1.0 and Analytics 2.0 concerns, touching on historic, real-time, and prescriptive insights. It also ties to the business performance of the enterprise. For example, when engaged in the planning and control of projects, it is important that managers develop plans in the context of the key performance indicators (KPIs) of the enterprise. KPIs are an important component of strategy development and implementation. In creating them, it is important that they reflect current and future project efforts, particularly when these efforts have a

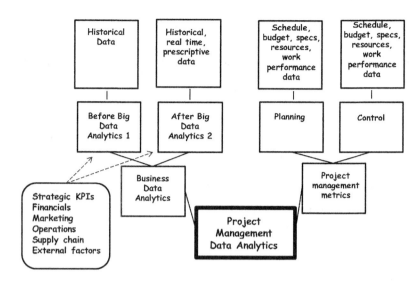

FIGURE 2.1
Project data analytics mind map.

significant impact on the long-term performance of the enterprise, e.g., in developing new products and addressing the rapidly evolving technology requirements facing the business. By the same token, it is important that the planning of projects addresses the enterprise's strategic direction as captured in KPIs. With project data analytics, KPIs and the project plan accommodate each other.

Other business concerns that should be accommodated include addressing the enterprise's financial performance and revenue goals, aligning projects with market needs, integrating project efforts with supply chain requirements, aligning projects with operations, and taking into account developments outside the organization.

DATA WAREHOUSING

In the 1950s, when computers enabled organizations to store data digitally, data was collected in a haphazard fashion. Accounting data was stored in distinct files simply as "accounting data." Purchasing data appeared in its own format. HR data was stored in a variety of formats (personnel, performance appraisals, salaries, timesheet figures, and more). The good news was that the computers were storing a vast array of valuable data that could offer guidance on improving organizational performance. The bad news was that in its present state, with formatting inconsistencies, the data was marginally usable.

The externally stored data evolved into what was eventually called a data warehouse. The process of collecting, massaging, and storing data became systematized. At the heart of the process was ETL (extract, transform, load). Data extraction (E) refers to the physical collection of data from different sources. Once collected, it needs to be transformed (T) into a format that enables it to be processed and analyzed. With Analytics 1.0, a substantial portion of the data analytics effort is dedicated to preparing data in a structured format for analysis. With Analytics 2.0, new advances in programming enable data collection and transformation to be carried out with reduced effort. The software can handle unstructured, voice, video, and social media data in addition to traditional structured data.

Finally, the L in ETL refers to loading (i.e., physical storing) of data in the database. The data should be stored in such a way as to optimize its retrieval.

Large construction and defense projects have employed integrated data for management and analysis purposes for decades. As long ago as 1978, the large American construction company Fluor reported that its key competitive advantage in executing very large projects was its electronic integration of project management methods into its construction practices (Baranson, 1978). Similarly, over the past several decades, the program offices of large defense projects have carried out highly complex projects using data that integrates project performance, supply chain, budget, and contract activities. Initially, the data integration entailed working with a patchwork of data bases, each using unique formatting conventions. But over the years, as computing power grew explosively and organizations became more sophisticated in handling very large data sets, data warehouses emerged that seamlessly integrated the data and enabled the execution of creative and powerful analyses that were limited only by the imagination of the analysts.

Figure 2.2 depicts a data warehouse configuration for a hypothetical project-based organization. Operational systems identifies the sources of data that will be put into the data warehouse. In the figure, this includes standard project data, as well as other categories of data that contribute to effective project data analyses (including data coming from the outside world). The raw data are massaged (through ETL) before being placed in a storage area (operational data store [ODS]). They undergo further massaging before being stored in the data warehouse vault. Once stored there,

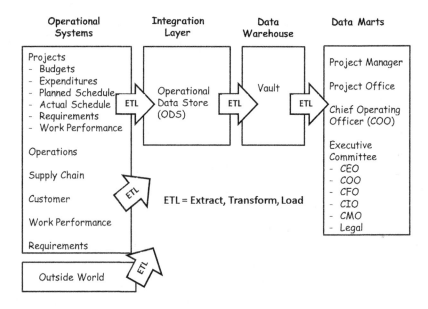

FIGURE 2.2
Data warehouse for a project-based organization.

they can be accessed by different marts, i.e., users who will employ the data for their specific decision-making purposes.

To appreciate the value of project data analytics to organizations, it is instructive to look at the value it offers to key players. Figure 2.2 identifies four of them: project manager, project office, chief operating officer (COO), and executive committee (comprising the chief executive officer (CEO), the COO, chief financial officer (CFO), chief information officer (CIO), chief marketing officer (CMO), and legal counsel). The actual players will, of course, be determined contextually and will vary from organization to organization.

Project Manager

The project manager's principal use of data will be to have a solid understanding of the project schedule, budget, requirements, and work performance. From the perspective of project planning and execution, this information provides the project manager and team with a detailed guidance on the work effort they need to carry out. From a control perspective, it enables the project manager and team to determine the extent to which the project is meeting the project plan. This type of information constitutes *descriptive analytics*, data that simply takes stock of a past or current state of affairs. The data can be tweaked in many ways in order to address different management questions of interest to the project manager. For example, a network diagram that is integrated with budget, contract, and supply chain data can allow the team to explore different performance outcomes associated with different cost, schedule, contracting, and supply chain scenarios. Thus the data can offer a view of alternative futures; in this case, it has *predictive analytics* capabilities.

Project Office

In many organizations, the project office is charged with supporting multiple projects. Project data analytics enables the project office to capture a big picture view of all project efforts carried out in the organization. It can provide important insights and guidance on project portfolio management. Looking beyond the activities of a single project, the project office can assess overall portfolio performance. It can identify possible portfolio imbalances and direct resources to specific projects to mitigate problems. It produces regular reports informing senior managers of project performance across the organization.

Chief Operating Officer (COO)

In many organizations, the enterprise projects are seen as a significant element of the organization's overall operations. When this is the case, it is important that the COO be apprised of the performance of the project portfolio. Of particular concern is the status of the largest, highly visible projects that have substantial strategic value. In one large American investment banking firm, whose project portfolio has $1 billion worth of projects, the project office provides the COO with monthly, one-page dashboard reports for the 300 top projects. The status of each project is identified as green, yellow, or red. Each month, the COO goes through the pile of reports in an hour, focusing special attention on projects with red or yellow status. At-risk projects, as well as those that may yield very high benefits, will be examined in more detail in follow-up inspections.

The dashboard contains data that is pertinent to assessing the status of a project, including

- Project status (green, yellow, red)
- Statement of business objective

- Business benefit
- Overall initiative timescale
- Estimated initiative cost
- Key players
- Project objectives
- Project time scale with key milestones
- Estimated project costs (in dollars, FTE, and level of effort)
- Major issues and risks
- Critical dependencies
- Changes
- Major accomplishments

During regular executive committee meetings, attended by members of the enterprise's most senior managers, the COO keeps other C-suite managers informed of the status of projects in the organization.

Executive Committee

In many organizations, the executive committee plays a central role in strategy formulation and execution. By establishing strategic goals, its members are able to define a roadmap the enterprise should follow to take it into the future. The goals cover all aspects of the business, including marketing, information technology, finance, operations, and legal. Achievement of many of the goals may require implementing projects. For example, through the strategy development process, the committee may reach consensus that in three years, 20 percent of revenue should come from new products that do not currently exist. These new products will be developed by means of projects. An examination of the current product and project portfolios provides business analysts with the information needed to identify new projects to put into the pipeline. This examination would focus on the composition of existing products in the product portfolio, new product development projects currently being undertaken, gaps in the product line that need to be filled, projected revenues associated with current and future products, personnel requirements needed to produce the new products, investment requirements to launch and maintain projects, and so on. The use of data analytics is central to the process.

A parallel strategic assessment of information technology needs and research and development (R&D) needs would also constitute an important component of the strategic plan. In the case of information technology

(IT), data on current IT capabilities are matched against a vision of capabilities needed at some future time, as defined by strategic goals. The development of IT solutions to address these capabilities will be carried out by means of projects, so the employment of project data analytics is needed to identify how the capabilities can be achieved through project management.

DESCRIPTIVE, PREDICTIVE, AND PRESCRIPTIVE DATA ANALYTICS

There are three broad categories of data analytics outcomes: descriptive, predictive, and prescriptive. While their goals differ, they hold one thing in common: each supports analysts in discerning meaningful patterns in the data being examined that can yield insights leading to effective action.

Descriptive analytics entails the collection and organization of data to describe a state of affairs of interest to an organization, including such things as the organizational capacity of an enterprise to carry out a large project (e.g., four data analysts are available; six are needed), the segmentation of a relevant market (e.g., the primary market comprises buyers between 25 and 30 years of age; our current product line is geared toward buyers >35 years of age), and the purchasing habits of the enterprise's customers (e.g., the data show that our product requires deliberate purchasing decisions that take time to make, typically two weeks; data show that our customers increasingly buy products on a whim). So with descriptive analytics, decision makers view the metrics to size up the current state of affairs, with the goal of discerning patterns that increase understanding and suggest action.

Analytics 1.0 is largely descriptive. As noted above, when project data analytics emerged in the 1950s and 1960s, attention was focused heavily on project planning and control when viewed from the perspective of the triple constraints: getting the job done on time, within budget, and according the specifications. The project plan was static and built around the project budget, schedule, quality factors, and specifications. It informed project executives of how much money the project would consume, the time it would take to do the job, the steps that needed to be taken to do the job, and what the deliverable would look like. Based on this information, decision makers could decide whether it was worthwhile supporting a project. Once a project was approved the plan provided a roadmap showing what work needed to be done. If the plan was changed, it would be replaced with a new static representation of the project.

An examination of the descriptive data can provide insights on how the future will play out, enabling descriptive analytics to become predictive. Consider an example from earned value analysis. Let's say a project is budgeted to cost $8 million (in earned value terms, budget at completion (BAC) = $8 million). A computation of work performance shows that for every dollar actually spent, 90 cents in value is achieved, yielding a cost performance index (CPI) of 0.9 (where CPI = (budgeted cost of work performed)/(actual cost of work performed)). CPI is a measure of the efficiency with which money is being spent to do project work. So if there is $2 million of work that needs to be carried out to complete the project, and 90 cents of value is generated for each dollar spent, the data suggest that it will cost $2.2 million to complete the project (($2 million)/0.9). The descriptive data provides an estimate of how much money is needed to finish the work. In this case, application of earned value management principles to the descriptive data gives you predictive data analytic capabilities.

Predictive analytics employs metrics to *predict* a future state of affairs based on the behaviors of subjects of interest (e.g., customers, employees, vendors, competitors) and trends in the organization, industry, or society. It is an important component of Analytics 2.0 and when employed effectively, it provides an organization with a competitive advantage. By detecting trends early, the organization is in a good position to prepare for future challenges. For example, the data may show that a company's customer base is gradually aging at a time that the market is being driven by the purchasing decisions of young people. Information like this can be used to adjust the organization's strategic vision, which in turn will drive changes in how it does business. Probably the best-known examples of predictive analytics today are metrics that capture the purchasing patterns of customers and can be used to target them when marketing products that align with the pattern. Amazon is a leader in employing predictive analytics this way.

With prescriptive analytics, analysts use data to provide managers with insights into how projects *should* be run to provide optimal results. Often, this entails modeling the project in some way and feeding different categories and levels of data into the model with a view of observing scenarios that predict alternative outcomes. For example, consider a company that is examining three different approaches to structuring a process for obtaining customer feedback regarding their satisfaction with enterprise performance. The process will be developed through project management. Let's say that three project models can be created, providing estimates for each project of the time and money that will be spent to deliver a solution. A comparison of the three approaches and their cost, schedule, and quality outcomes will highlight the most cost-effective approach to employ.

Increasingly, as hardware and software technologies advance at breakneck speed, new methods of handling complex data—comprising enormous data sets, structured data, and unstructured data that includes unstructured text, audio, visual, and social network data—are emerging. ETL is being compressed so dramatically that experts predict that the use of data warehouses for supporting data analytics will be replaced with real-time, instant analysis of data. This leads us to the question: Are we moving into a new data analytics stage—data analytics 3.0?

DATA ANALYTICS 3.0?

Davenport argues that beginning in the mid-2000s, Analytics 3.0 emerged (2013). To him, what distinguishes Analytics 3.0 from its predecessors is its focus on embedding data collection and analysis capabilities in products and services. For example, using sensors to stream information from turbines, jet engines, and medical imaging devices, GE identifies the servicing needs for these machines. Another example is UPS generating data to monitor all aspects of its package delivery service, enabling it to implement actions through analytics that lead to cost savings, speedier deliveries, and increased customer satisfaction. After installing sensors in more than 46,000 company trucks, UPS developed the ability to guide drivers' pick-ups and deliveries in real time. The cost savings of analytics-driven operations at UPS have been substantial, for example, saving millions of gallons of fuel each year. The effect of embedding data collection and analysis in products and services is to make them more intelligent.

It is argued here that Analytics 3.0 extends beyond embedding data capture and tracking capabilities in products and services. Just as the shift from Analytics 1.0 to Analytics 2.0 was triggered by technological advances, coupled with radically changed ways of looking at business operations, we see these same factors causing a qualitative change in the practice and outcomes of data analytics, yielding a shift from Analytics

2.0 to Analytics 3.0. Consider the following advances in technology that impact how data analytics can be employed:

- Real-time tracking of trillions of data points, yielding near-instant assessments of what is transpiring, and driving appropriate actions to handle the situations being addressed. The most dramatic advances in this area are for military purposes, e.g., tracking terrorists by monitoring the full range of electronic communication across the globe. Real-time tracking of such a large data set requires data extraction, transformation, and analysis to occur so quickly that, practically speaking, actionable results are produced instantly.
- *Artificial intelligence that can be used in all aspects of data analytics.* AI can be applied to determining what data to extract, identifying data patterns, devising strategies for filtering data in order to focus only on pertinent data, drawing conclusions from an assessment of the data, surfacing optimal strategies to act upon the information received and analyzed, and more.
- *Machine learning.* The pinnacle of AI applications is the creation of machines that replicate human thinking processes (Casola, 2017). The ability to handle very large data sets through increased hardware and software capabilities is bringing us closer to producing the thinking robots portrayed in science fiction movies. Currently, much of the development effort in this area focuses on "training" machines to formulate and solve problems by providing them with examples of thinking process they should be able to apply to produce actionable results. Scientists and engineers have now created the first machines that can teach themselves how to solve problems without human intervention. For example, AlphaGo is a software routine that provided the rules of the game of Go, and from those rules, created millions of problems to solve, learning game-winning strategies along the way (Temming, 2017). It can beat the human world champion.

ONCE AGAIN: WHY DATA ANALYTICS IN PROJECT MANAGEMENT?

This chapter has provided a nutshell review of the evolution of data analytics, with a focus on its use on projects. The overview shows that the employment of data-rooted metrics on projects extends back millennia. Broadly speaking, project management has been data-driven from the start. However, the recently coined term "data analytics" goes beyond the mere application of data-rooted metrics on the job. In recent years, a data analytics paradigm has arisen that focuses on the conscious and systematic employment of data to support management decision-making. This perspective coincided with the advent of computers in the workplace in the 1950s. The capacity for computers to store large amounts of potentially useful data was immediately evident among managers. The challenge was to devise ways to format, store, and retrieve data to make it useful in offering actionable solutions to problems. As hardware and software technologies moved forward, the capabilities of data analytics and its contribution to addressing a broad range of complex issues grew remarkably, reaching the point today where it seems possible to know everything about everything.

Employment of data analytics has value for all categories of projects, because decisions made on all projects must be informed by data to the extent possible. This includes projects that are large, medium, or small; high-tech or low-tech; those that deliver service solutions as well as those tied to the production of tangibles; complex or simple projects; projects in the public sector as well as the private sector. Having said this, it is clear that the type of analytics that can be employed productively varies substantially according to project context. There are no one-size-fits-all solutions. With very large projects such as those carried out in the defense sector, as well as commercial projects that entail manipulating petabytes of data, advanced Analytics 2.0 perspectives and methods are de rigueur. With small, simple projects, the low-end methods of Analytics 1.0 will likely be satisfactory. But whether the executed projects are characterized as low-end or high-end, a number of points relevant to the implementation of project data analytics should be taken into account:

- Project data analytics should go beyond focusing narrowly on the triple constraints. It should also encompass the business needs and activities of the enterprise and should accommodate pertinent factors from the outside environment.
- Traditional project planning and control concerns should be informed by data analytics efforts designed to address the specific circumstances of individual projects. That is, project planning and control need to adopt a data analytics perspective.

- People assuming project data analytics responsibilities should become fully immersed in current data analytics practice; they should have a solid grasp of basic statistical and modeling principles so that the work they carry out produces useful, valid, actionable results.
- If the data analytics effort is deemed important to the organization's functioning, the organization should adopt a data scientist job position, to be filled by individuals who play an important role in the data analytics effort. These individuals should have statistical and modeling skills, and should also have good data processing capabilities to handle the challenges of extracting, transforming, and loading data so that it is formulated in a way that supports effective analysis.
- The project data analytics effort should be aligned with business strategy and should contribute to its formulation and implementation.
- Organizations that routinely carry out more than two or three projects should adopt a project portfolio outlook that enables the data analytics effort to address the enterprise's entire project management initiatives holistically.
- For most organizations, it makes sense to place the project data analytics function in the project management office. If an organization has a corporate-wide data analytics capability, the project management office should play a lead role in aligning project data analytics with the enterprise's corporate data analytics perspective.

So why data analytics in project management? Because it leads to data-driven decision-making that yields superior project outcomes, and because it requires projects to operate outside the narrow confines of traditional project management practice with its focus on the triple constraints, enabling them to be an integral part of the business.

REFERENCES

Baranson, J. *Technology and the Multinationals: Corporate Strategies in a Changing World Economy*, Lexington, MA: Lexington Publishers, 1978.

Casola, L. *Challenges in Machine Generation of Analytic Products from Multi-Source Data: Proceedings of a Workshop*, Washington, DC: National Academy of Sciences, 2017.

Davenport, T. H. "Analytics 3.0," *Harvard Business Review*, 2013.

Stapleton, L. K. "Big Data," *developerWorks* (IBM), 2011.

Temming, M. "Computer Learning Game with No Help: Alpha Go Devises Strategies Unknown to Human Players," *Science News Magazine*, 2017.

3

Data Analytics Risk: Lost in Translation?

Carl Pritchard

CONTENTS

As organizations become more and more reliant on data for decision-making at virtually every level, the effort becomes a search for information and a journey to convert that information into business intelligence. But the quest for trends and patterns can be rife with risk. In order to generate a level of honesty and validity, the key is to be aware of what's real and what's assumptive. Before having an effective risk management conversation in the data analytics space, the key is to know what types of information you seek and the perils associated therewith.

THE RISK MANAGEMENT PROCESS

No matter the professional arena, the risk management process is relatively static. Risk tolerances are established, and risks are then identified and assessed. Once the higher priority risks are known, it's possible to determine strategies that are appropriate.

Data analytics is seen in many spaces as the perfect breeding ground for negative risk outcomes. Individual and corporate bias may skew the data. Ineffective data collection can cause weak interpretations. Data security and privacy create an inherent level of potential problems. Data sources and cultural influences can drive effective interpretations off the proverbial cliff.

Any effective process needs to begin by identifying what can and what cannot be tolerated. Establishing tolerances sounds easy, but it's actually more complex than might be imagined. Can the organization tolerate unplanned data release, data manipulation, or data breach? If the initial response is *no*, then re-evaluate the question by asking if a single file out of millions suffered any of those conditions, would it still be intolerable?

Tolerances are points beyond which an organization will not go. Staggeringly, most organization have not invested time or energy in establishing those points. There are no clear lines. As a result, individuals make their own assumptions about how and where the lines should be drawn, creating an environment of potential threats generated by the individuals working on our data. If each individual draws his or her own lines, then there is no true management of the risks.

ESTABLISHING TOLERANCE

Tolerances are well established when there are unambiguous statements about the organizational posture on data, for example, "a single manipulated file is one file too many." Such hardline statements clarify where the organization is risk-tolerant and where it is risk-averse. Without clarification across the data analytics project or across the organization, individuals will take it upon themselves to apply their own risk attitudes, creating an environment where risk management becomes random at best (Figure 3.1).

Within Tolerance (Risk-Prone)		Exceeding Tolerance (Risk-Averse)
Where we *will* go...		Where we *will not* go...
-We will investigate a single manipulated file		-We will shut down if two or more manipulated files are discovered
-We will not fire staff over a single phishing incident	T O L E R A N C E	-We will fire staff over a repeat phishing incident
-We will allow a variance from real data of 0.01%		-We will not allow a variance from real data of > 0.01%
-We will allow data release before the final scrub, but only after it has been reviewed by at least three staff		-We will withhold all data that has not been reviewed by at least three staff

FIGURE 3.1
Establishing tolerance.

Because tolerances are born out of experience, as organizations discover new challenges (and failings), they have the opportunity to clarify a new what tolerances we should worry about and represent the risk posture of our organizational culture.

Tolerances also serve to drive the organization to focus on specific risk categories that represent areas of serious concern to the integrity of our data and our interpretations of the data. In many ways, tolerances reflect who we truly want to be in the realm of data analytics. Sadly, most organizations do not clarify (at least publicly) what they will or will not tolerate as an organization. Instead, they will wait until untoward events transpire and then declare those events unacceptable. Truly risk-aware organizations apply those tolerances before the projects even begin.

Interestingly, there are no right or wrong answers in the realm of tolerances. Instead, there are test environments. If a tolerance is declared, and the acceptability of outcomes proves to be undesirable, it's time to move the limits. But if no tolerances are declared, in a very real sense, everything (and nothing) becomes acceptable.

There is a close relationship between risk governance and data governance, as both represent the creation of rules, processes, and cultures in regard to what are and what are not acceptable behaviors. The tedious task of creating policies for data collection and preparation is akin to any effective risk management practice. And a key component of all of these practices is the creation of risk and data analytics language.

RISK AND DATA ANALYTICS LANGUAGE

How high is "high risk"? How much data is "enough"? No matter the environment, the definition of terms drives the ability to understand whether or not our management practices serve the organization's best interests (Figure 3.2). As a manager, if you want to control risk in your environment, controlling the language is a powerful early step. In the late 1990s, there was a huge conflict associated with the decennial census of 2000, as the Census Bureau made the argument that a valid statistical sampling of the U.S. population would be just as valid as a full enumeration. The arguments channeled their way through dozens of different bureaucracies, culminating in a lack of a resolution (and ultimately, a full enumeration of the population). The challenge was not associated with whether or

Establishing Risk Impact Levels

- High – Requires immediate management attention and/or intervention (e.g., could cause long-term injury or death)

- Low – Can be dealt with at a team member level, requiring updates only through regular reporting channels (e.g., the customer will never notice and it is reparable)

- Moderate – Between high and low

FIGURE 3.2
Risk and data analytics language.

not statistical sampling was a valid practice. Generally, everyone accepted that it is. The challenge came with definition of terms. And the term that caused all the furor was "valid." That single adjective, undefined, rang the death knell for a statistical analysis of the population.

In our data gathering, many of the arguments can be rendered moot if the terms associated with our practices are defined long before any interpretation of the data is underway. By defining the terms earlier, rather than later, there's a much higher probability that the interpretations will be deemed valid, as those terms are not serving the perceived bias of the moment.

The same principles apply in risk. If the terms are established early, any challenge that we are too risk-averse or risk-tolerant is quickly wiped away. The first individual or group to establish the terms generally wins any arguments, as late-comers are often seen as shifting terms for the sake of their own agenda.

Once the risk culture has been established (or at least ground has been broken), organizations can move forward with the true business of managing risk.

DATA COLLECTION RISK

The big questions in data collection are:

- What data do we need?
- For what purpose?
- What forms and formats?
- From what sources?
- Using which techniques?

For any one of those considerations, there are risks.

WHAT DATA DO WE NEED AND WHY? (RISK #1—THE NEED)

The operative word here is "need." The nature of the data needs is a source of risk. Do we need 10 samples or 10,000? Do we need current, real-time data, or will history serve? Will the data be used to establish preliminary steps or as the final verdict?

The key in dealing with data needs from a risk perspective is to establish the need. This means identifying the absolute maximums and minimum in terms of the data sets required. It means ensuring that the data needs to align with the desired outcomes. It means ensuring that sources exist for the data and those sources will continue to exist for a sufficient time that supplemental data retrieval will be possible if required.

Establishing needs is more complex than it might sound. Needs are things that are required. Without the need being fulfilled, the data analysis cannot move forward. In some analyses, only a handful of data points are required in order to establish trends and clarify information. In other analyses, large volumes of data are required to achieve the same goals.

Thus, one of the first risks that any data analytics project faces is the risk that the true needs have not been identified. There is the risk that too little data is demanded to meet the need. There is the concurrent risk that not enough data is specified to meet the need. Like Goldilocks, the key is to determine the volume of data required to be "just right" for the analysis in question. A failure to determine the true need creates the potential impact of invalid (or too expensive) analysis. Both can ultimately spell failure for the analysis.

IS THE DATA PROPERLY SOURCED? (RISK #2—THE SOURCE)

Josiah Stamp served in the British Civil Service in the early twentieth century, and during that time, he established a principle known as "Stamp's law" based on his interpretation of data-gathering in India at that time. "The government are very keen on amassing statistics. They collect them, add them, raise them to the nth power, take the cube root and prepare wonderful diagrams. But you must never forget that every one of these

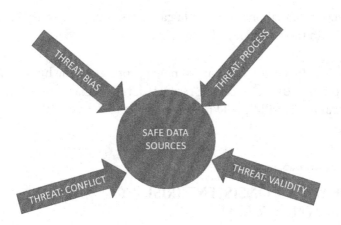

FIGURE 3.3
Sample impact levels.

figures comes in the first instance from the chowky dar [night watchman in India], who just puts down what he damn well pleases."

Stamp's law points to the second major risk associated with data analytics. The source may be in the right geography and may generate numbers that fit flawlessly within the data set, but the source itself may lack validity (Figure 3.3).

In valid analytics, while the source may be outside our sphere of control, its integrity must be beyond reproach. When it comes to human factors, the individuals should be evaluated for potential bias. When it comes to mechanical or electronic inputs, the systems generating the data need to be double-checked to determine if they have the true capacity to generate requisite data on a consistent basis in a consistent form or format. In determining if the source is valid, several basic questions can clarify whether or not there is "source risk":

- Where was the data published? Was it published in a journal of repute or by an association with a clear bias?
- Who paid for the data? If the data was paid for by an organization seeking a specific outcome, the source may be held in less esteem than if it was paid for by an organization with no vested interest in one perspective or another.
- Are the processes for data collection clearly stated in the publication? If there's a lack of clarity on how the data was collected, there's a very real possibility that the sources may be called into question.

- Do the affiliations of the data gatherers count? Are they recognized within their field of endeavor?

The more of those questions answered appropriately, the higher the probability that the data sources are respected, thus enhancing the likelihood that the analysis will be held in esteem.

IS THE DATA CONSISTENT (RISK #3— CONSISTENCY RISKS)

Another risk consideration in data collection is the degree of consistency with the data involved. This definitely does *not* mean that all of the data needs to have a consistent set of values, but it does mean that the data needs to reflect consistent sourcing, consistent integrity and consistent quality. If 80% of the data is derived from validated, legitimate sources, but the remaining 20% could readily be called into question, then consistency is going to potentially generate significant risk to the overall acceptability of our data. Any aspect that might call into question the apples-to-apples validity of the data calls all analysis into question.

This also ties significantly to forms and formats for the data in question. Data storage, retention, and retrieval protocols can become touchstones for questions regarding the consistency of the underlying data, not just its storage.

Consistency is also an issue associated with any data profiling activity. In examining existing data sets to determine if they have cross-applications, two additional risks can readily surface. The first is the accuracy of the profile in using the existing data set for alternative purposes. By sometimes shoving the proverbial "round peg" in the square hole, data intended for one purpose may be a force fit, but it may also succumb to misinterpretation or misuse. Either situation can cause a degree of inconsistency that renders the later analysis moot.

The second additional risk actually manifests in the form of threat and opportunity. Data profiling occasionally provides early warnings about the challenges associated with data gathering on a particular data type. In highlighting these challenges, there may be a temptation to alter the data collection process to learn lessons from past mistakes. While such risk aversion may be laudable, it may also cause some inconsistencies in approach as data gathered before the lesson is learned may not align with data gathered after the warnings reach the light of day.

RISK COLLECTION

One particular type of data collection that needs to occur outside the specific framework of the project in question is that of risk collection (aka, risk identification). Risks are identified based on personal and organizational experience, and the more personal and organizational experiences that can be brought to bear, the better the chance that a meaningful set of risk data can be amassed. The basic rules for effective risk identification are the following:

1. Engage as many *meaningful* stakeholders as practicable.
2. Get participants to participate consistently.
3. Keep the focus on the mission.

Engage Meaningful Stakeholders

In gathering data, there are sources, analysts, and end-users. In identifying risk, the insights of personnel from each of these perspectives are vital. To minimize or ignore any significant subgroup creates a situation where significant risks may unintentionally be overlooked. Those from the sourcing perspective, for example, likely understand when data-sharers may be liberal in their willingness to dole out data and when those same sharers may wax reticent. Knowing those organizational and environmental cues can point to where the probability of high-quality data increases (or decreases) dramatically.

Gather Risk Insight Consistently

"Weather" is not a risk. "A thunderstorm may cause a power surge, leading to data corruption." That's a risk. What's the difference? If we explain risks *and their impacts* in full sentences, we have the opportunity to understand the genuine concern associated with a given risk event. What's the bad thing that may happen? What's the impact it may cause? Anything less leads to free-floating anxiety, rather than risk analysis. It's relatively easy to identify risk sources or categories of risk. It's much more challenging (and healthy) to identify the specifics that cause us concern and lead to a clearer understanding of the directions we need to take.

Focus on the Mission

Without a clear direction, risk identification can run amok. The challenges stem from a tendency during risk identification to delve into risks well beyond the data, its sources and the processes to be applied in the analysis. Identification can stray into all aspects of the data's ultimate applications and the environments in which the data will be applied. Identification can lead to a repository of every element of angst for every stakeholder, rather than a focused analysis of what might go wrong in the data analytics.

It's a problem that's readily solved. Every time the question, "what are the risks?" is raised, the question should be raised as, "what are the risks associated with the data collection, analysis, process, and interpretation?" Simply reframing the question often eliminates the inherent tendency to stray.

EXPLORATORY VS. CONFIRMATORY VS. PREDICTIVE

The question may also be framed against the intentions for the application of the data. Is the data collection effort (and subsequent analysis) designed to be exploratory, confirmatory, or predictive? Each of these carries with it inherent risk, but in different areas and in differing degrees.

EXPLORATORY RISK IN DATA ANALYTICS

Exploration carries with it an inherent risk. Just as explorers took grave personal risks seeking new frontiers, data analysts take extraordinary risk to find and interpret data. And the nature of the risks are inextricably wed to the nature of the exploration. Just as the first explorers to the New World had a less-than-stellar survival rate, those conducting exploratory data gathering face significant peril. The nature of the risks in exploratory data analytics stems, not surprisingly, from the unknown. Since both the nature of the data and its potential interpretations are not preordained in exploratory analysis, surprises may abound. Among them

- lack of data availability,
- lack of data integrity, and
- lack of data cohesion/trends,

to name but a few.

AVAILABILITY

In exploratory data collection, the nature of the desired data may be crystal clear, but the data may simply not exist. Even if the data sets can be developed, the process of unearthing them can lead to a skewed analysis, since the lack of any available pool of data can lead to a very small sample set. While a small sample set may have statistical significance, it may not be sufficient for later, larger-scale interpretation.

Availability issues can also lead to the misidentification of data as germane to the research. The old Japanese proverb, "when you're a hammer, all the world's a nail," applies here as well. Thin data pools can lead to a lot of "nails," or misidentified data. In attempting to minimize exploratory data analytics risk, it's important to clarify, in advance, what good data look like (versus bad data).

INTEGRITY

To understand integrity issues, one need look no further than the contentious environment between those who subscribe to anthropomorphic climate change and those who do not. Many of the arguments from climate change skeptics actually stem from questions regarding the integrity of the data being applied in these aspects of science. Terms like "adjusted data" or "imputed data" lead some parties to label the data as lacking integrity. Why the doubt? Because the skeptics contend the data could not be accurately replicated and is inherently inconsistent.

In situations where we have the capacity to replicate the data and ensure it can be re-applied and re-used, and that fresh data can be drawn from the same sources, there is true data integrity. If we have data integrity, the impacts of data loss or corruption are significantly reduced. In terms of risk mitigation, few aspects of data analytics are more significant than any systems that ensure high degrees of integrity.

EXPLORATORY TRENDS

Risk in establishing trend information is generally associated with reading too much or too little into the trends. In exploratory analysis, the key is to ordain, as early as practicable, what will constitute a trend. That's much easier said than done and requires a risk mitigation strategy of multiple perspectives. If a single individual or organization makes the determination on what constitutes a trend, the analysis will inherently be skewed.

CONFIRMATORY ANALYTICS RISKS

Many of the same considerations apply in confirmatory analysis, but the risks are dramatically lower. Because all of the same considerations are in play with an emphasis on affirming a given premise, the risks drop because the number of variables is somewhat reduced. Some of the baseline assumptions for confirmatory analysis negate some of the more obvious risks and their impacts.

DATA AVAILABILITY

In a situation where we are working to confirm a premise, it's far more likely we know what data will serve us in that regard. If we know what data we're looking for, we can then more readily ferret out the sources for that information. Since the premise is in place, it's also likely that we have a clear sense of precisely what data will and will not fit into our models. As a result, availability risks are significantly reduced vis a vis exploratory analytics.

DATA INTEGRITY

In many confirmatory analytics situations, the premises have already been researched in earlier forms and formats. As such, identifying data that will or will not conform to our models is more readily achieved. As with data availability, risks are reduced. However, data integrity here can also be somewhat deceptive. Just because a data source has proven effective in the past, there's no guarantee it will continue to be effective in updated research and analysis.

DATA TRENDS

Past Performance Is Not Inherently Indicative of Future Results

Time and again, brokerage firms remind their clients of that timeworn adage. It's particularly applicable in confirmatory analysis. The efficacy of past analyses does not guarantee that current analyses will bear out the same results. And if there is too great a focus on repeated results, it's possible that the risk of misinterpretation will be increased, rather than decreased by the familiar.

PREDICTIVE RISK IN DATA ANALYTICS

Data analytics is the modern-day "crystal ball" used to provide guidance on everything from crop planting to satellite launches. The risks associated with predictive risks are not generally seen as being in the same family as the risks in exploratory and confirmatory data analysis. That's a mistake, as all of those risks exist here just as realistically as they exist in the previous two categories. Most of the risks perceived in predictive risk stem from the relationship between those risks already identified and the nature of uncertainty.

Uncertainty is the degree to which we have any sense of the probability of possible outcomes. The key is to understand the degrees of uncertainty that exist in any given environment. The most common example is tomorrow's weather forecast. If the meteorologist announces that there's a 75%

chance of rain for your community tomorrow, the key is to know what that prediction means and what it's based on. The first step is to know what you're identifying.

Some people make the mistake of assuming that a 75% chance of rain means that three-fourths of the region will receive rain and one-fourth will not. Still others assume that it means that the forecasters have a 75% confidence level in the impending rain. The reality is born out of data analytics. A 75% chance of showers means that 75% of the time the weather models have looked the way they look right now, rain has ensued. The data taken into account include wind patterns, pressure systems, humidity, temperature, dew point, wind speed, and a variety of other variables. Put all of those variables into play in a predictive model, and (when conditions are what they are now) 75% of the time it will rain.

Weather predictions are an ideal example, as most people hear them all the time, yet very few people genuinely understand what they're being told. Weather predictions are also ideal, in that they point out the key risks associated with predictive analytics.

THE FUTURE IS UNKNOWN

Until 2012, most people in the Midwest and Mid-Atlantic had never heard the term *derecho*. It refers to a line of powerful, near-hurricane-force storms that begin small and build into a powerhouse capable of generating billions of dollars in damage.

Derechos had never been a common weather feature for the Midwest and Mid-Atlantic. While northwest Arkansas anticipates at least one derecho a year, most of Maryland and Virginia sees one every four years, and because of the nature of the storms, they were not commonly labeled as such. Thus, in 2012, when the derecho began back in Illinois and Indiana, there was no general alarm. By the time it had passed, it was the largest nonhurricane weather event in Virginia history, and ten Virginians had lost their lives.

As Nassim Taleb points out in the book *The Black Swan,* black swan events (those with no past history) aren't predicted until after they happen. The future is unknown. As a result, in any predictive analysis, caveats about the comprehensive nature of the data must abound. To fail to acknowledge that outside unknown influences may alter the interpretation of any predictive data set is folly.

THE FUTURE ENVIRONMENT IS ONLY
PARTIALLY KNOWABLE

A search for bad predictions on the Internet turns up a host of technology examples. Predictions that Apple would never make a phone and that the Internet was a passing fad were based on the understandings of existing data. The current environment will change. That's the single certainty. Time and again over the last 50 years, we have been warned of the imminent collapse of fossil fuels and their *certain* unavailability. If the technologies for extracting those fuels remained the same and no more fuel had been discovered, those predictions might have become true.

The environment changes. That constant change means that predictive analytics need to capture not only the data sets, but the environment in which those data sets evolved. Assuming there will be no change in the environment creates an inordinate amount of risk.

In 1968, *Time* magazine made the clear and simple prediction: *remote shopping, while entirely feasible, will flop.* In 1968, there was no Internet. There were no cell phones. Color TV was still a relative novelty. Technology, by today's standards, was extraordinarily limited. The authors of the article relied on the data sets that were readily available at the time. And they used that environment to make their predictions.

Imagine how much more prescient they would have appeared if they had said, "Given today's technologies, remote shopping will flop. Should there come a time when catalogs are wired between the home and store and when the store can deliver more efficiently than picking it up by oneself, remote shopping could become a very real possibility." Part of predictive analytics is simply acknowledging those elements of the environment that have a direct influence over our predictions.

PREDICTIVE ANALYSIS AND CONSEQUENCES

It's notable that even in ancient Biblical times, analysts were making predictions. And false prophets were killed for bad prophesies. In modern times, analysts make predictions, and the best analysis includes the "if accurate/ if inaccurate" set of outcomes. This is a critical risk mitigation approach to ensure that the implications of the analysis are fully understood.

Air pollution statistics in the late 1960s showed the Industrial Revolution had led to lower air quality and higher incidence of lung disease in major metropolitan areas. Some believed the findings. Others did not. But Richard Nixon was ultimately able to create the Environmental Protection Agency. The analyses of his day were bolstered by the notion that if the data were accurate, quality of life would continue to degrade. And if the data were inaccurate, the worst that would happen is that cities would have less grit and ash in the air. Both outcomes, regardless of the data, were positive. It allowed those who believe the data to accept the views of those who did not. It's a classic example of how an examination of the consequences can reinforce the outcomes, regardless of the data.

RISK IN COMMUNICATING RESULTS

In classic children's storytelling, the "Boy Who Cried Wolf" repeated his fearmongering time and again. And when he really needed protection from the wolf, no one believed his argument. It's a cautionary tale that would serve any data analyst well. In data analytics, the communications channels we establish and the means by which we share our messages need to be carefully considered if we are to avoid the boy's lupine fate.

When to Share

Data analytics can be exciting. The trends discovered, the outcomes realized and the insights garnered can reveal hitherto misunderstood or unknown information. In our fast-paced society, the desire to be first with information can be overwhelming. The second person to market with information will quickly be forgotten. Thus, there's a compulsion to share information as soon as it appears to be valid. Validity in analytics is elusive. Wait too long for too much data, and the analyst runs the risk of being considered an also-ran. Release trends too early with too little data, and the analyst runs the risk of being considered premature and the data invalid.

Many of the old journalistic mantras may apply on sharing data. When there are multiple respected and named sources declaring the information valid, it's good for release. When the data tells a clear, indisputable story, it's good for release. When the data sources are backed up and repeatable, it's good for release. All of those criteria should be met before we begin sharing the data.

How to Share

The sheer volume of data sometimes makes it impossible to share all of the data collected. The issues of intellectual property also create their own morass of risk. The risks associated with the "how" go to the perceptions of the data shared and how it ultimately will be interpreted.

To the degree acceptable (for the organization that generated the data in the first place), the first question is how much information can be shared without giving away intellectual property. A somewhat simplistic solution is to share the outcomes or insights generated by the data supported by a representative sample of the data in question. The outcome statement minimizes the risk of others jumping to their own conclusions about our data. It also provides a sense of the original intent of the research when it began. The representative sample of the data illustrates how conclusions were drawn without encouraging or forcing others to work through the detailed analyses that we have so painstakingly conducted. The sample data minimizes the potential challenges to our data set, our data collection practices and our interpretation. It limits the risk generally associated with data exposure.

With Whom to Share the Message

As the message is shared, it's important to limit risk by sharing insights with the appropriate parties. While it could be argued that anyone should be able to accept a well-constructed data set and its conclusions, that would be a utopian ideal. The reality is that virtually any analyses have their detractors and those who come to the table with a set of preordained conclusions. They challenge data not on its merits, but on principle. Such a mentality creates a high-risk environment, as it is not the data under scrutiny, but the ideas behind the data.

The higher the degrees of data source validity and data integrity, the lower the risk from such situations. But if the sources and integrity of the data are even marginally questionable (or are polluted by the actions of poor data practice), the risks of sharing insight with the wrong parties grow exponentially. The only mitigation strategy in such situations is to return to the data sources to ensure the outcomes are repeatable and that the data has integrity. If the data or its sources are in any way corrupted, the risk of misinterpretation is very high, and it may be time to reassess whether or not the data is ready for release.

SOLVING AND RESOLVING OUR DATA ANALYTICS RISKS

This discussion is rife with references to mitigation strategies. Virtually every standard practice in any field of management endeavor is prone to risks and risk management. From the forms and templates used to capture data to the standard the look-and-feel of graphic outputs, each represents someone's resolution to a perceived threat to their efforts.

In proactive risk management, the key is to have the strategies in place and in play before the risks are ever realized. The axiom that "an ounce of prevention is worth a pound of cure" applies here. Efforts to select the right risk strategies should incorporate a high level of pragmatism. Any time someone suggests an approach to ameliorate our risks, we should ask three basic questions:

- Will it work consistently?
- Does it generate more harm than good?
- Does it allow for the same outputs as other data in the analysis?

Will It Work Consistently?

An effective risk management strategy is not a one-and-done proposition. It is a strategy that can be applied in a given set of circumstances and repeated. As long as the circumstantial environment is the same or highly similar, the strategy should be capable of being applied and re-applied. This is the reason that so many templates and forms take root in organizations. Each is seen as a risk strategy in its own right, and thus becomes part of the consistent practice that renders the organization risk-capable.

The most effective way to identify strategies that won't work in the long term is to identify strategies that are intensely situational and that require tweaking throughout implementation to keep them valuable. If a strategy to minimize risk requires more effort than the data gathering itself, there's an inherent problem.

Does It Generate More Harm than Good?

Is the cure worse than the disease? That's a fair question when it comes to the solutions we identify for data analytics risks. If the risk approach creates a situation where the data may be called into question, it's not an ideal strategy. It the risk responses create new risks in the visibility of trends or the integrity of the data, they are not ideal strategies. If the responses are seen as clearly deleterious to the data as a whole, the responses should be shelved.

While this may seem obvious, during risk-response development, some individuals and organizations become possessive and obsessive about their strategies. As such, they find it hard to see the potential harm that may be done to the original analyses *by* the strategies. In order to overcome these potential problems, other stakeholders should participate in the process to provide perspective on the viability of the strategies being deployed.

Does It Allow for the Same Outputs as Other Data in the Analysis?

Templates for data capture are risk responses. The templates ensure that bad data doesn't seep in and that forms and formats are consistent. But they can also eliminate certain data from the data set that doesn't conform to the form or format. That can prove problematic. The nonconforming data may be an indicator. And if we can't see it, we can't take it into account. In our zeal to ensure that data is pure as the wind-driven snow, there's a distinct possibility that we may create a situation where some of the data may be missing from our analyses.

SUCCESS!

Success in risk management is not when all of the risk is eliminated. Success is when the risks are managed to acceptability. That acceptability may come in the form of acceptable data, acceptable analyses, or acceptable outputs. If the risk tolerances are well defined, if the risks have been identified by a cross-section of stakeholders, and if the risk strategies pass the simple litmus test above, not all risks will be eliminated. But they will be managed.

4

Analytical Challenges of a Modern PMO

Seweryn Spalek

CONTENTS

Projects have a nearly five-thousand-year history. Some argue that they back-date to ca. 2600 BCE (Before Common Era), when the pyramids were constructed during the Old and Middle Kingdoms of Egypt, or at least as far back as the building of the most significant parts of the Great Wall of China, which occurred during the Imperial China Period under its first emperor, Qin Shi Huang. However, the shaping of the systematic way of managing projects that we know today began in the 1950s. The major projects at the time were military ones, associated with the Cold War period. A special imprint on modern project management development was made by the projects involving the U.S. Air Force's missiles, National

Aeronautics and Space Administration (NASA) space program, and U.S. Navy submarines. It was during this period that the program evaluation and review technique (PERT) and the critical path method (CPM) were invented.

In this context, the history of project management offices (PMOs) doesn't look so impressive as the first organizational entities of that type were created some twenty years ago. As a core concept, they were supposed to help deal with new challenges associated with the rapid increase in the number of projects run by companies. At the time, many of the PMOs were cancelled within a couple of years after their initiation. The author's worldwide study, conducted on more than 400 PMOs in 2010, revealed that 88% of cancelled PMOs did not survive beyond a four-year period and were mainly eliminated due to the lack of the PMO's ability to show any value added to the organization. Executives' expectations toward PMO outcomes were very high, but those expectations were not operationalized. They were defined as a general vision for increasing project or program efficiency. This could be taken to mean that more projects would be on-time, within budget, and within scope. It could also mean better procedures for gathering data on project status or setting up and enforcing project management standards. However, the abovementioned study revealed that, during the startup process of PMOs, the scope of their activities wasn't clearly defined. Therefore, the success criteria couldn't be established effectively with which to evaluate achievements. Moreover, from the very beginning, PMOs started to be labeled differently by the organizations they operated within. With their studies, Hobbs and Aubry (2008) revealed that some examples of PMOs' names were project management office, program management office, project support office, project office, project management group, project management center of excellence, directorate of project management, and that these offices served different roles and functions. After its formative years, the PMO concept matured and evolved toward a general understanding, which was mostly related to its level in the organization and the scope of its responsibilities. Therefore, today we have PMOs that could be at the program or project, departmental or portfolio, or enterprise level. Their scope may range from supportive to decision-making, from administrative to active, from single project management to a full portfolio. Moreover, a PMO can be created within a company or as an outsourced entity. The latter is mostly associated with temporary PMOs, which are usually created for the purpose of extensive programs. A typical example of a project with a temporary PMO is the construction of a factory or power plant, while permanent PMOs are mostly created to serve an organization that runs numerous concurrent projects.

For the purpose of further elaboration, we will mostly focus on PMOs that are described as entities permanently located within an organization's structure and serve the purposes of more than a single project. However, some of the findings could also be useful for large programs consisting of projects.

Irrespective of their future type, the first PMOs were created to fulfill the need to gather data from single, typically large, projects in order to better control implementation. Moreover, the records of completed projects could be analyzed and used in the planning processes of forthcoming endeavors. As a result, the major PMO function was to endorse the best practices to follow and set up project governance standards for the organization.

With the increasing number of projects run by the organizations, the functions and roles of the PMOs evolved as well. The PMOs emerged with new sets of responsibilities, beginning with project management staffing and career paths. That meant dealing with a new type of data in the area of human resources associated with projects. That ability soon became crucial, especially in terms of information and communication technology (ICT) projects, in which the shortage of experienced project leaders presented specific challenges to software companies.

With the advent of the current century, the number of projects soared and continues to do so, and these projects no longer operate as separate endeavors. They influence and interact with each other in a dynamically expanding fashion. As in the jungle, they very often need to share the same resources, which are limited not only within the company, but on the market, as well. They compete for funds, are under constant time pressure, and more frequently need to react to changes in their clients' requirements. In this environment, project managers without analytical support are doomed to fail like the lonely hunter in the jungle (Exhibit 4.1). Last, but not least, this complicated, multidimensional situation generates another set of data, which should be managed somehow, but by what entity? The most natural entity would be PMO, presenting an analytically comprehensive challenge.

EXHIBIT 4.1
The project manager without analytical support is doomed to fail like the lonely hunter in the jungle.

Source: **Image used under license from Shutterstock.com. Author: YuanDen.**

TOWARD AN ANALYTICALLY MATURED PMO

Each company should increase its level of maturity in project management over time. That is not a choice nowadays, but a must, in order to survive in today's aggressively competitive market. It is the only way to deliver a product or service faster, with lower costs, and better fitted to, or even exceeding, the client's needs. Reaching the next level of maturity means a higher awareness of choice in the project governance strategy of the company. That strategy should describe when, and to what extent, the company is going to use a traditional or agile approach in managing projects. In doing so, the company may consider applying a hybrid project management approach. This concept has been gaining in popularity recently, especially outside of the IT realm. It assumes that, in waterfall projects, some elements of agility are introduced. An example of such a project could be a hoover, which, at a basic level, is a typical engineering product whose development was, until now, done as a typical waterfall project. But, if it is to be made into an autonomous device, implementing the traditional project management approach would take a lot of designing and preparation time. In contrast, when the agile approach is used for the autonomy-related issues of the project, the product should be ready earlier and better fitted to the client's needs. This is because, by working in an agile way, closer to the client's sets of requirements, we can more quickly decide which requirements are the most important to the user, implement them, and then show them to the client for approval. Of course, that also means that the client and project teams must be ready to work in a highly interactive, agile environment. Therefore, reaching higher levels of maturity in project management also means evolving toward a unique approach to meeting the client's expectations and establishing a specific level of trust in order to fully implement agile methods, in practice. However, this can be more easily achieved if the PMO is able to present reliable data sets from already completed projects, done in both the traditional and agile ways. This will support the development of the vision for the next level's maturity achievements.

As a result of multidimensional analytical requirements, modern PMOs should gather data from four major areas:

- Methods and tools
- Human resources
- Project environment
- Project knowledge management

In each area, we should be able to assess the ability of a PMO to analyze data. The level of this ability should be described as *analytical maturity*, following the general concept of maturity in organizations or the concept of capability maturity model integration (SCAMPI, 2006). The typical maturity assessment level ranges from 1 to 5; where 1 represents the lowest and 5 the highest level of maturity. The description of analytical maturity levels is given in Table 4.1.

TABLE 4.1

Description of the Levels of a PMO's Analytical Maturity

Level of Analytical Maturity	Description
1	The data is not gathered by the PMO in any systematic way. If any data is collected, it's the result of legal requirements or imposed by single project documentation purposes.
2	The data is gathered sporadically and ad hoc by the PMO on demand. Due to data incompleteness, analytical abilities are very limited. The PMO may present only fragmentary results of the data analysis.
3	The PMO has some established procedures for gathering and storing data. Once stored, the data is analyzed only occasionally or upon specific request. The results may be presented in a more comprehensive way.
4	The data is gathered, stored, and analyzed in a systematic way, according to PMO needs. The results of data analysis cover the full range of project outcomes in the company.
5	The PMO seeks continuous improvements in its analytical abilities towards better alignment with the company strategy.

METHODS AND TOOLS

In order to successfully run projects, a PMO should establish an effective method for project governance, define the standard for managing projects, and endorse a set of tools to be used. This can be achieved by adopting one of the widely recognized standards, such as PMBOK® (PMI, 2017a), PRINCE2®(AXELOS, 2017), or ICB® (IPMA, 2017). However, if an organization is going to increase its maturity level in terms of managing projects, there is usually a need to modify a recognized standard or even to build one from scratch. To achieve this end, the PMO should be able to analyze the data and show in which areas the adopted standard fully fits the specifics of the projects run by the company. Moreover, it should recognize the places in which there is a need to modify an approach, or even work out a completely new approach, to managing the projects in the organization. Let us examine, for the moment, the case in which a well-established producer of refrigerators decides to digitalize its products. The idea is that, by adding a computer-type unit with a display on the front doors, the client could be advised in many aspects. First of all, it can review the recipes that may be chosen in respect of the contents of the fridge. Second, it can give advice on which products need to be stocked up on. If the producer decides to connect the fridge to the Internet, the device can even order some goods from an online store. What is a dream for the marketing department could be a nightmare for the project or product managers. Trying to utilize the same standard for developing the fridge and enhancing its IT capabilities would be a disaster. Further, the development of IT functionalities using a waterfall approach would take too long. If the producer applies a detailed planning phase, the completely designed IT product would already be outdated before its production even starts. That is because IT tools and techniques evolve so quickly that the only way to follow them is to deliver the product on an incremental basis. Therefore, the PMO for this producer should first try to gather data on similar projects from the market and then analyze them. If no data or limited data is available, then a pilot project should be run using an adaptive or agile approach and data carefully gathered from the moment of its implementation. The data should then be analyzed with a view to finding the best standard that matches the IT fridge development needs. Once this standard has been chosen, the solution should be implemented. However, this does not mean that the data analysis process should be ended. On the contrary, data should be continuously gathered to modify the newly adopted standard for IT fridge developments. Furthermore, it is up to the PMO to gather necessary data from different approaches of managing the IT fridge development project, analyze it, and propose the methods and tools that are the most efficient for that type of project. Moreover, even if the IT fridge project looks easy for software developers familiar with the agile approach, it has very innovative areas that should be managed using, for example, the extreme project management approach. One of those areas is the object sensor system that recognizes the items that are placed inside the fridge. The other could be a secured Internet application for buying the goods from an online store with home delivery. The third area could be a system that collects data from the household (family) and smartphones on their daily physical activities. Data collected concerning these areas could then be used to propose suitable door displays for the fridge, including, perhaps, personalized diets based on daily activities or lack thereof. Applying hybrid project management, the producer could effectively produce the hardware (fridge) in a traditional way and IT (digitalized fridge) by applying the agile approach. This example shows how much data from different sources must be analyzed by a PMO in order to establish an adequate standard for managing projects in a company nowadays. In addition, even when the project has been completed, there should be a continuous effort to increase the maturity level in that area. Even at the fifth stage of analytical maturity (see Table 4.1), there is an ongoing analytical effort to follow changing market trends.

HUMAN RESOURCES

According to the Project Management Institute (2017b), the shortage in the number of professionals who have experience in and knowledge on how to manage projects will continuously increase. The reason is that the number of projects is increasing very rapidly in global terms from year to year, whereas the number of project managers who enter the market do not make up that gap. Even if universities and training companies are doing their best to graduate more and more students, this will still not be enough. Moreover, pure knowledge is not enough to create a valuable worker. Mastering project management takes time. Some people argue that the widely known rule of 10,000 hours to proficiency (Ericsson et al.,

1993) is not accurate, as there are people who learn faster and those who learn more slowly. However, if we assume those 10,000 hours are correct for the majority of individuals, it will take roughly 5 years (if one spends 8 hours per working day practicing only project-related work) after graduation to become an experienced project manager. Furthermore, increasing the number of students also takes time, and universities can only estimate how many students will be necessary in the next 5 years. That creates additional inertia, as this is akin to predicting, say, how much of a specific wine strain or single malt whisky you need to produce now to completely fulfill demand in, say, 10 years. In order to deal with the shortage of experienced project managers, we should be able to categorize projects in some fashion. In practice, not every project requires extensive expertise in managing projects. Some of them require good organizers, some strong leaders to follow, and some simply facilitators. It all depends on the type of project, and its size and complexity. If the project is already well-defined, but is large and complex, it would be better to assign to it an experienced professional. Therefore, the modern PMO should be able to categorize different types of project according to the skills required by the project managers. Good examples would be the construction of a new power plant or a newer version of an aircraft. Those types of projects are more likely to require a deeper knowledge of the standards used in managing projects in a traditional way. On the other hand, designing the shape of a brand-new car or starting a new web-based service requires more flexibility than extensive scholarly knowledge and hours of expertise. In those cases, it is more important to assign managers and team members to the projects who have problem-solving orientation, are innovative, and have a willingness to closely cooperate with other people. In some cases, there is even no need to have a project manager. For example, in agile projects that run according to the Scrum approach, there is the position of Scrum master, which is not that of a typical project manager. Sometimes, the leaders of agile teams are called agile project managers, but a more adequate name should be facilitator or coach, and the first of these will be used henceforth.

All of this means that the PMO should have additional roles besides its traditional function of staffing, training, and dealing with the career paths of project managers. The PMO should be able to create a requirement matrix for both projects and team members (including project managers or facilitators). This matrix should be based on the data gathered and analyzed from concluded and ongoing company projects and different types of team members that could be found on the market or inside the

TABLE 4.2

An Example of a Requirement Matrix for Project Types and Team Member Requirements Based on Data Analyzed by the PMO.

		Type of Project			
		Fridge With New Engine	IT-Enhanced Fridge	New Web-based Services	Construction of New Factory For Fridges
Staff requirements	Experienced Traditional Project Manager				✓
	Experienced Facilitator			✓	
	Traditional team member	✓			✓
	Agile team member		✓	✓	
	Project Leader				✓
	Project Manager	✓		✓	
	Facilitator		✓		

organization. Data should also be gathered from sources external to the company, based on the market research conducted. Therefore, for example, a crowdsourcing idea could be used, as well. An example of a requirement matrix geared toward project management skills and expertise is shown in Table 4.2.

The creation of a proper staff requirements matrix is not an easy task. In practice, this means that the PMO must gather data from inside and outside of the organization. It should then have the ability to analyze the data and create a matrix that is unique to the organization.

PROJECT ENVIRONMENT

In the past, the project's environmental considerations (if any) were limited to two major factors, political and economic. Nowadays, the number of sources of data from the environment is much larger, and these sources come from three major areas: external to the organization, within the organization, and at the project level. At first, technology-related issues were added as a result of the implementation of lean product management and the just-in-time approach. That created new dynamics in engineering systems. The project managers started to be aware of issues related to the latest technological progress, and the company's awareness of being a part of the wider business ecosystem went down to the project level. This means that a new expectation appeared in the form of project managers having to consider the influence of competitors' activities. Former enemies on the market became quasi friends. That created a completely new dimension of external project environment management. Previously, the project manager had to be aware of and cooperate simultaneously with other project managers within the organization. Nowadays, the set of foes and allies managing other projects has expanded close to the company's borders. The question in the minds of project managers has now become: how to acquire information about these managers? And the answer must be delivered through the PMO, which should be the eyes and ears of project managers. The data analysis done by the PMO should be able to spot the potential areas of cooperation and threats. Finally, under the pressure of the public and some nonprofit organizations, considerations of the social and environmental impacts of projects began to be included in management issues. This trend was so strong that it evolved over time into the corporate social responsibility (CSR) management concept, influencing each project through its organization's external commitments.

Therefore, nowadays, the project environment external to the organization includes politics, the economy, technology, competitors, and CSR. Within the organization's internal environment, we should distinguish company policies and organizational culture, quality assurance systems, the number and availability of resources, organizational structures, and maturity, while, at the project level, the crucial issue is the interactions between key players within the project, program, or projects in the PMO portfolio. Issues, such as the ethics of workers and personal interests, which are often not in line with each other very often, need to also be considered. With the increasing number of projects run by the companies, cooperation between such projects is more often replaced by competition. Therefore, if we should even start to talk about the coopetition among projects and identifying possible areas of cooperation and competition, then we will need data analyzed by the PMO. Only with this knowledge will we be able to manage conflicts and enhance the synergistic effect of cooperation in order to achieve higher efficiency in the entire project ecosystem. Moreover, each of the environmental areas mentioned is not as stable as it used to be. Therefore, the PMO should have the ability to gather up-to-date information about the directions of changes in each of the environments, analyze them, and predict the possible impact on the project's outcomes. That means a massive amount of data has to be first gathered from different sources, and that task alone is a great challenge for a modern PMO. Furthermore, that data needs to be validated, especially the external section, and analyzed very carefully using rigid statistical methods. A mistake in this process could lead to highly negative consequences, not only for single projects, but for the PMO's portfolio, or even the organization, at large.

PROJECT KNOWLEDGE MANAGEMENT

The project knowledge management concept has been of increasing importance during recent years and will continue to be even more so in the future. In the author's studies, conducted in the years 2010–2014 on 675 PMOs worldwide (46% European, 28% North American, 18% in Asia and the Pacific, 11% in South and Latin America, and 9% in the Middle East and Africa), it was revealed that nearly 50% of PMOs have tried to manage project knowledge in some fashion. Those attempts were, of course, of different types and scopes, but they showed that the PMOs had noticed the importance of these issues in increasing the efficiency in managing projects. When those trials were not successful, PMOs did not give up, and almost 40% of them declared the need for managing project knowledge in a systematic way. However, it must be noted that the amount of prospective data that can be transformed into knowledge is soaring from year to year. This causes a situation in which we know theoretically how to deal with project data, but turning the ideas into practice is extremely difficult. It is worth mentioning at this point that the increasing gap between the theory and practice of knowledge sharing is not only a project-related issue but has wider connotations and implications (Dalkir and Liebowitz, 2011).

It is important to understand that project knowledge is related to one of three levels: individual (project managers, project team members, facilitators, product owners, sponsors, clients, and so on), project (including programs and portfolios), or organizational (companies, NGOs, universities, and so on).

In general, we can distinguish between explicit and tacit knowledge. The project and organizational levels are more about explicit knowledge. This means that a PMO should have access to the data associated with standards and policies established within the organization. From the projects and programs perspective, a PMO should gather data from previous endeavors and firstly analyze it with a view to applying it in forthcoming projects. That data should also be analyzed with respect to challenges coming from projects that could be described in a systematic way, in order to avoid these same challenges in future projects. Portfolio data analysis should be used to create knowledge of the business value of projects. This knowledge can be used in the forthcoming portfolio-building process to choose projects that better fit the company's strategy and create more value added. Last, but not least, the data should be stored and analyzed for future usage on an individual level, which is described further on.

The most demanding task for the PMO is to identify, collect, and store tacit knowledge, which is very often hampered at the individual level. To collect the data associated with that type of knowledge, a different approach must be followed. The PMO should create a system that endorses the revealing of data by individuals in exchange for additional benefits for themselves. It sounds easy in theory, but it is very difficult to implement in practice. Companies that have tried to implement such a systematic approach very often did not achieve their objectives. The employees weren't motivated enough to reveal their secret information as the trade-off was not attractive to them. The difficulty in creating an effective trade-off system lies in the different motivations of individuals and even cultural issues. Sometimes, the issue is in the technical way of collecting that knowledge. Some individuals prefer face-to-face exchanges, while some are more happy to relay knowledge using computer systems or the pen-and-pencil approach. Moreover, the physical location of data collection points is important, as the companies' environment is not always friendly enough. In that case, it is advised to promote remote systems of data collection, which may be used at home or in other, more convenient locations. Therefore, if a PMO would like to create a systematic approach to tacit knowledge exploration, it must be multidimensional. Some companies have tried to implement a knowledge-dollars (k$) system to endorse tacit knowledge sharing by individuals. The idea is very simple. Each individual receive k$ (similar to loyalty programs, e.g., run by stores or airlines) for sharing their knowledge. In most cases, those k$ are to be exchanged for some good and this is far from being enough. Such simple systems usually die (stagnation has been observed in the data collection process) after a couple of months. If we expect the system to work in the long term, it should not be limited to tangible benefits but should also consider intangible appraisals. Moreover, it should also facilitate the grapevine sharing effect toward capturing the tacit knowledge associated with these. Therefore, the benefits system should consider financial bonuses, rewards, gifts, and excursions, as well as nominations for prizes, endorsing team building, team meetings, and informal talks. However, the PMO should also work on increasing the awareness of individuals on the importance of data sharing for themselves, the project, and the entire organization.

It must be clearly stated that an effective approach to project knowledge management must be accompanied by an efficient system of data identification, collection, and storage. Only proper analysis of that data leads to transforming raw information into knowledge that can be utilized in projects, as shown in Figure 4.1.

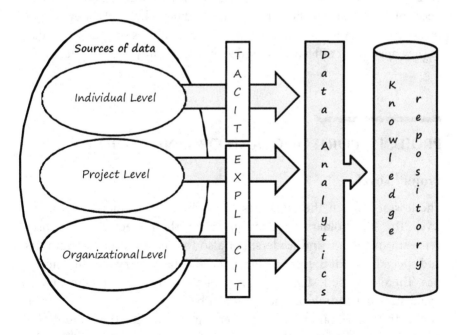

FIGURE 4.1
The process of transforming project data into knowledge.

THE PMO AS THE MULTILEVEL DATA ANALYSIS CENTER

Based on the abovementioned author's studies on more than 400 PMOs worldwide, the most desired PMO roles were: (1) setting up and enforcing standards/methodology/templates, which was pointed out by 65.9% of respondents, showing how important and valuable applying knowledge on project management is for companies; (2) reporting (gathering data on project status), which was indicated by 65.7% of respondents; (3) project or program portfolio management (prioritization of the projects), which is a significant topic for any company operating in the multiproject environment, with 51.1% of respondents; and (4) as a data repository (access to historical data and lessons learned), which was declared by 29.5% of respondents.

It is remarkable that, among the different roles, the PMO should serve as a source of information for so many players in projects. Among them are project managers, project leaders, project coordinators, technical staff, engineers, project managers, program managers, portfolio managers, project directors, executives, and other stakeholders. Therefore, it is crucial to manage the data flows and analytics according to the different needs of identified stakeholders, which could be individuals or even organizations. However, each function or position requires various sets of data as they operate on different levels, depending on the project's outcomes.

PROJECTS, PORTFOLIO, AND ORGANIZATION

Project Level

The lowest level in the outcomes hierarchy is the project or program level. The stakeholders there are primarily the project manager, project team members, and leaders, but also the technical staff, engineers, and specialists. All these individuals need data to carry out their activities. Therefore, the PMO should, first of all, deliver action plans, which could vary depending on the approach being applied to project governance. In traditional project management, the expectation is to deliver a detailed plan of activities connected to individual workers. The plan must include such data as the start and completion dates of the task, assigned resources, and the scope of work. For project managers, leaders, and some specialists, the plan should include budgetary information, as well. With that data set, the workers can do their job based on their knowledge, skills, and expertise. However, in order for the workers to perform their tasks more efficiently, it is desirable that the PMO provides them with data on similar tasks performed with lessons learned. Moreover, the PMO should be able to provide, upon an individual's request, any additional data that they need to conduct their tasks with higher efficiency. For example, the PMO's analytical tools should be able to support problem-solving on the part of individuals. Furthermore, the PMO should collect data concerning progress on tasks and their completion. Individuals should be able to report any issues, and the ways that they resolved them (or not!) to the PMO. Unresolved issues should be analyzed and compared with data from other projects to check to see if there were similar problems and how they were resolved. If there has been no resolution to date, the issue should be designated for further analysis with an open status.

Portfolio Level

In the middle, or portfolio, level, projects or programs that fulfill similar business needs are put together. The data gathered from individual projects, after analysis, should allow an assessment of the status of the entire portfolio in terms of achieving portfolio objectives. That data also allows projects to be prioritized according to their importance in fulfilling the objectives of the portfolio. Individuals needing data at that level are those working as portfolio managers, project directors, or in similar positions. The PMO should also provide these individuals with data associated with the company's strategy. Based on the PMO's analysis, the goals for the entire portfolio should be set up. On a regular, or even an on-time basis, the performance of the portfolio should be checked in relation to the business needs of the organization. The data on the outcomes delivered by the portfolio must be addressed in relation to the data for assumed goals. In the case of any differences between those two sets of data, the portfolio manager should be notified immediately. It is advised that the PMO should create a synopsis table showing the health status of the portfolio based on the analyzed data, as shown in Figure 4.2.

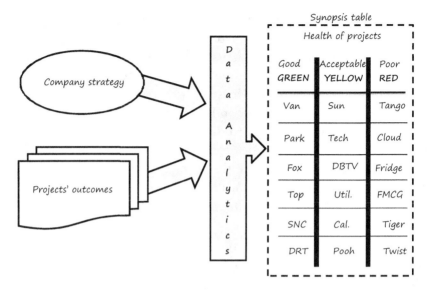

FIGURE 4.2

An example of a synopsis table of the health of projects based on data analysis.

Organization Level

At the highest, or organizational, level, data should come in the form of mainly portfolio level. However, in certain cases, the PMO should be able to, upon request, present data from the program or even project level. The PMO should prepare a report on the health of the key portfolios in the company on a regular basis. The recipients of that data should first be the executives and project and portfolio managers.

On that level, a similar synopsis table as that for projects should be created. The difference is that, based on the data from the portfolios, the health status of the portfolios should be assessed. In addition, if there is a portfolio whose performance is poor, then a second layered, in-depth analysis of the data from projects included in that portfolio should be prepared. However, if that happens, in addition to executives, the portfolio managers should be notified. The result of data analysis from endangered portfolios should be recovery plans. Those plans, thanks to the advanced analytical tools available, should propose different scenarios for troubled portfolios or even projects.

In addition to the projects' outcomes levels, in each organization, it is possible to distinguish three separate levels associated with the decision-making process: operational, tactical, and strategic.

OPERATIONS, TACTICS, AND STRATEGY

Operational Level

At the operational level, workers perform their jobs on a daily or weekly basis. In the agile approach, that can even be down to hours. The project staff make their decisions towards short-term plans, and they deal with the project requirement changes as they receive updated plans progressively as well. In traditional project management, the changes can also be in task duration and budget. The agile methods are much more flexible to changes. However, there is a need to convert the client's strategy into daily actions through so-called user stories. In order to do so, additional data analytical feedback from the PMO may be useful. The project staff mostly report the data on the progress of the work in relation to deadlines, scope, and budget in waterfall projects. In an agile approach, a report is more about achieved goals in relation to the client's expectations and team performance indicators such as, for example, its velocity. The project managers and Scrum masters also report any issues related to achieving short-term goals to the PMO.

Tactical Level

Based on the information received from the strategic level, the PMO, after analyzing them, prepares the data sets required to achieve medium-term goals at the tactical level. This level is of special importance for traditionally managed projects. In the agile approach, there is, in fact, no need for this level as a direct link between strategy and operations should be constructed. The program or portfolio managers should plan, on a monthly or quarterly basis, which goals should be achieved. Based on that, specific data is worked out for the operational level. The PMO should also gather the data related to the accomplishment of the medium-term tasks, analyze them, and prepare adequate information for the next, or strategic, level. Moreover, the PMO should analyze the issues reported at the tactical level, resolve them, and, if necessary, elevate some to the strategic level. The PMO should also have the authority to assign additional funds or reallocate existing funds among projects. Upon request, the PMO should also have the ability to agree on new completion dates and scope changes. However, all those changes would have to be done within boundary lines previously agreed to by executive decision makers on the strategic level. Therefore, the PMO should be able to analyze the data to check that none of the project's staff has exceeded his or her authority.

Strategic Level

The highest level of executives oversee projects from a yearly or longer perspective. Therefore, the PMO should analyze the data from the lower levels of execution and present it to the executives in such a way that they can make key, long-term decisions. At this level, the PMO should also address any issues related to significant time, budgetary, or scope changes, especially in the portfolios of projects or programs. If necessary, the PMO should provide any additional data needed to make the decisions necessary for the future of seriously challenged projects. It is up to the PMO to provide, based on data analytics, different scenarios for struggling endeavors. Those scenarios may include additional funds, time, or even termination of the projects. Each of these scenarios should consider the possible long-term consequences for the organization. The strategic level is crucial for both traditionally and agilely managed projects. However, in agile project management, as mentioned, a direct link to the operational level should be established. The strategic data should be analyzed and converted to support the decisions of the agile teams in their daily operations. Moreover, the data from all agile projects should be collected, analyzed, and presented at this level for executives to make a strategic decision for the entire organization. This approach creates advanced flexibility in the organization's decision-making processes and is a result of being closer to the clients needs than ever before. That is because the customer, being actively involved in the work of agile teams, expresses their requirements. Furthermore, those expectations can be recorded on a daily or weekly basis and, after being collected from different projects, can be analyzed and compiled as reports presented at the strategic level. The most valuable are analyses showing shifts or sudden, unexpected turns in clients' requirements. These could form the basis for future market trend predictions. However, being closer to the clients' expectations and having the data on that more quickly transported to the highest level, creates new challenges for the implementation of the augmented analytics approach to the organization (Cearley et al., 2017).

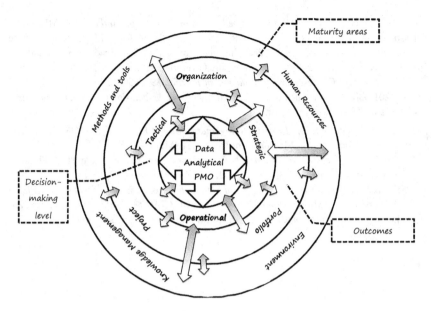

FIGURE 4.3
Analytical challenges for the PMO based on the data flows from different sources.

The Challenge of Multi-Sourced Data

As has already been explained, the PMO must deal with massive amounts of data coming from different sources. The summary of these previous elaborations is shown in Figure 4.3.

The PMO's analytical abilities should be able to combine the data from all areas to better support decision-making processes in current and forthcoming projects. However, the picture of data sources, as described in Figure 4.3, will definitely evolve over time. That is an additional challenge for a PMO. If a PMO would like to effectively embrace this evolution, it should have built-in agility, as well. Only in being adaptive to changing analytical requirements may the PMO present the value added it should create in that demanding area of expertise.

REFERENCES

AXELOS. (2017). *Managing Successful Projects with PRINCE2*®, First Edition, Second Impression: TSO (The Stationery Office), Norwich.

Cearley, D. W., Burke, B., Searle, S., & Walker, M. J. (2017). *Top 10 Strategic Technology Trends for 2018:* Gartner.

Dalkir, K., & Liebowitz, J. (2011). *Knowledge Management in Theory and Practice:* MIT Press.

Ericsson, K. A., Krampe, R. T., & Tesch-Romer, C. (1993). The Role of Deliberate Practice in the Acquisition of Expert Performance. *Psychological Review,* 100(3), 363–406.

Hobbs, B., & Aubry, M. (2008). An Empirically Grounded Search for a Typology of Project Management Offices. *Project Management Journal,* 39, S69–S82.

IPMA. (2017). ICB – *International Project Management Association Competence Baseline,* version 4.0. Nijkerk: Author.

PMI. (2017a). *A Guide to the Project Management Body of Knowledge (PMBOK® Guide),* Sixth Edition: Project Management Institute (PMI).

PMI. (2017b). Project Management Job Growth and Talent Gap Report//2017–2027. Newtown Square, PA, USA: Project Management Institute.

SCAMPI. (2006). *Standard CMMI Appraisal Method for Process Improvement (SCAMPISM) A,* Version 1.2: Method Definition Document. CMU/SEI-2006-HB-002. Retrieved January, 2018, from www.sei.cmu.edu/library/abstracts/reports/06hb002.cfm.

5

Data Analytics and Project Portfolio Management

Alfonso Bucero

CONTENTS

What gets measured, gets managed.

—**Peter Drucker**

INTRODUCTION

Organizational growth usually results from successful projects that typically generate new products, services, or procedures. Top managers aim for better business results. Managers are increasingly aware of the need to do projects, programs, and operations to transform their strategy into execution. Management is usually concerned about getting optimum results from the projects under way in their organizations and also by collaborating across the organization. Projects seem to be unlinked to the organizational strategy, and project managers are unaware of the quantity and scope of the projects.

When a survey was conducted in several organizations about assessing their project environment, one common answer was found: "We have too many projects."

When analyzed, some of those projects were not needed for the organization. Then, selecting projects based on their strategic importance helps resolve such feelings. But top managers need to be aware that projects are the means of converting strategy into execution. The common goal is to fulfill the overall strategy of the organization. Usually all projects draw from one resource pool, so they share some common resources.

On the other hand, to be able to select the right initiatives to be converted into portfolio components (projects, programs, operations), some historical, environmental, economic, ethical, or other type of data need to be used, and it is when "data analytics" starts playing in the game. Executives want better ways to communicate complex insights so they can quickly absorb the meaning of the data and take action. Over the next two years, executives say they will focus on supplementing standard historical information with new approaches and point of view that make information come alive. Those new approaches may include data visualization and process simulation as well as text and voice analytics, social media analysis, and other predictive and prescriptive techniques.

Regarding the term, "data analytics" usually refers to a variety of applications, from basic business intelligence (BI), reporting and online analytical processing (OLAP) to different forms of advanced analytics. It is similar in nature to business analytics, another global term for approaches to analyzing data, with the difference that the latter is oriented to business uses, while data analytics has a broader focus. The wealthy view of the term is not universal, though. In some cases, people use data analytics specifically to mean advanced analytics, treating BI as a separate category.

Data analytics initiatives may help businesses increase revenues, improve operational efficiency, optimize marketing campaigns and customer service efforts, respond more quickly to emerging market trends, feel safer as organization, and gain a competitive advantage over rivals. Depending on the particular application, the data that was analyzed can consist of either historical records or new information that has been processed for real-time analytics uses. In addition, it can come from a mix of internal systems and external data sources. As soon as organizations start using data analytics, executives and board of directors begin to ask themselves if they are obtaining total value from their initiatives on data analytics.

Data analysis is important part of an executive's agenda, board of directors, clients, and, importantly, business investors. Furthermore now, more than ever, organizations are focused on data analysis to make better decisions and to figure out what their investment portfolio should be. The use of data analytics has been generalized; important business organizations are now starting to adopt data analytics as a concise strategy, and not as a dispersed set of technological projects.In this chapter, the relationship between project portfolio management (PPM) and data analytics is explained to offer a clearer and understandable perspective to executives in organizations to make better decisions for projects, programs, and organizational success based on a more clear, concise, and accurate data.

PROJECT PORTFOLIO MANAGEMENT AND DATA ANALYTICS

Over the years several organizations were consulted on project portfolio management and when some customers were asked why they wanted to implement a project portfolio management (PPM) solution, the main reason was usually to gain visibility into their data so they could improve decision-making. They are wondering, how can we make PPM data analytics easier? Analytics and reporting is the right way to get visible data.

The general consensus from customers was while they loved the wealth of data available to them, they had many ideas on how they could make it easier to use the data more effectively.

These ideas may be broken down into three core themes:

- *Simplify*: make the data easier to access and manage;
- *Unify*: provide the analytics where the customer is working;
- *Provide self-service*: give users the reports they need, when they need it, so they don't have to request the report and wait for someone else to make it available.

In our superfast business world, data analysis and data visualization are really important. In the realm of PPM, organizations need robust data analysis to make better decisions and improve strategic execution.

The key is to have the right processes in place to collect the right data and ensure that the data is of good quality. As had been said before, data gathering is not free; any data that is collected but not actively used is a waste of organizational resources. Knowing what information is needed to drive better decision-making will help ensure that only important data is collected. Therefore, organizations need to wisely consider what metrics, analytics, and reports are most important to senior leaders and then develop or improve the processes that drive the gathering of that data. The power of having good portfolio data is to conduct a better portfolio optimization.

Levels of Analysis

Once organizations have a stable foundation for PPM data collection, they can move forward to the data analysis journey. Three levels of data analysis can be distinguished:

1. Descriptive analysis
2. Predictive analysis
3. Prescriptive analysis

Descriptive analysis—this helps answer the question, "What has happened?"

This level of analysis is the foundation as it is fact-based and is required for developing key performance indicators and dashboards. It is the transformation of raw data into a form that will make them easy to understand

and interpret, rearranging, ordering, and manipulating data to generate descriptive information.

In descriptive data analysis, some possible questions to interpret raw data are such as the following:

- How often does each value (or set of values) of the variable in question occurs? For example, how many and what percentages?
- Which number best represents the "typical score"? For example, how similar are the data?

Descriptive analysis focuses on the exhaustive measurement of population characteristics. You define a population, assess each member of that population, and compute a summary value (such as a mean or standard deviation) based on those values.

Predictive analysis—this helps answer a more important question, "What will happen?"

With sufficient data, organizations can begin to predict outcomes, especially related to project risk and project performance and the impact to project delivery as well as the portfolio as a whole.

Predictive analysis is often defined as predicting at a more detailed level of granularity, for example, generating predictive scores (probabilities) for each individual organizational element. This distinguishes it from forecasting. For example, predictive analytics is the "technology that learns from experience (data) to predict the future behavior of individuals in order to drive better decisions."

In future industrial systems, the value of predictive analytics will be to predict and prevent potential issues to achieve near-zero breakdown and further be integrated into prescriptive analytics for decision optimization. Furthermore, the converted data can be used for closed-loop product life cycle improvement, which is the vision of the Industrial Internet Consortium.

Prescriptive analysis—this helps answer a more difficult question, "What we should do?"

This requires more detailed and advanced analysis to determine the optimal path against a set of potential choices. Prescriptive analysis of the portfolio provides significant benefits by enabling organizations to choose the highest value portfolio and choose a group of projects with a higher probability of success.

Prescriptive analysis not only anticipates what will happen and when it will happen, but also why it will happen. Further, prescriptive analytics suggests decision options on how to take advantage of a future opportunity or mitigate a future risk and shows the implication of each decision option. Prescriptive analytics can continually take in new data to re-predict and re-prescribe, thus automatically improving prediction accuracy and prescribing better decision options. Prescriptive analytics ingests hybrid data, a combination of structured (numbers, categories) and unstructured data (videos, images, sounds, texts), and business rules to predict what lies ahead and to prescribe how to take advantage of this predicted future without compromising other priorities.

Table 5.1 summarizes the different types of data analysis, with each of them answering different questions, and they have a different purpose, and they cover different functions. This table is also identifying who is the responsible or owner to do it.

TABLE 5.1

Analysis Type

Analysis Type	Question Answered	Purpose	Functions to be Covered	Responsible
Descriptive analysis	What has happened?	Establish current state performance through historical business analysis	• Dashboard/KPI development • Performance benchmarking • Insights/segmentation • Fact-based assessments	• PMO • Data analyst • PPM responsible • Business managers
Predictive Analysis	What will happen?	Predict outcomes, propensity, customer behavior, preference, or entity	• "What-if" marketing scenario development and forecasting • Predictive classification of risk, behavior, or outcome	• PMO • Data analyst • PPM responsible • Customer feedback
Prescriptive analysis	What should we do?	Analytic methods to show implication or impact of a series of decision options	• Simulate organizational financial/ops impact across a series of strategic options • Develop optimal path against a set of potential choices	• PMO • Data analyst • PPM responsible • Finance

Portfolio optimization is one of the main parts of the prescriptive analysis described above. Organizations should endeavor to get to this point because it delivers important value and significantly improves strategic execution. In order to optimize any part of the portfolio, organizations need to understand the constraints that exist (e.g., budgetary, resource availability, ethical, political, and so on).

These restrictions are the limiting factors that enable optimal scenarios to be produced. There are four basic types of portfolio optimization:

1. *Cost-value optimization*: This is the most popular type of portfolio optimization and utilizes efficient frontier analysis. The basic constraint of cost-value optimization is the portfolio budget.
2. *Resource optimization*: This is another popular way of optimizing the portfolio and utilizes capacity management analysis. The basic constraint of resource optimization is human resource availability.
3. *Schedule optimization*: This type of optimization is associated with project sequencing, which relates to project interdependencies. The basic constraints of schedule optimization are project timing and project dependencies.
4. *Work type optimization*: This is a lesser known way of optimizing the portfolio, but corresponds to a more common term, portfolio balancing. The basic constraints of work-type optimization are categorical designations.

Approach

Figure 5.1 summarizes the above points and highlights how having the right data inputs combined with constraints and other strategic criteria can produce optimal outputs across four dimensions of portfolio optimization.

To apply a five-step methodology for conducting analytics is suggested, which enables organizations to realize the full potential of their analytic processes:

- *Define*: Determine the performance criteria for measuring PMO/PPM success and develop a set of questions and hypotheses for further modeling and investigation.
- *Adapt*: Gather and transform all available resource, project, and business data for further visualization and analysis.

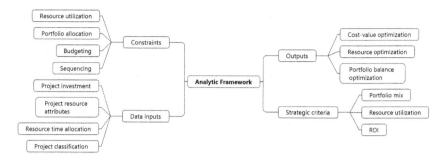

FIGURE 5.1
Analytic framework.

- *Visualize*: Inventory all projects with related resources and highlight key trends and insights based on project and business data.
- *Assess*: Develop analytic framework to test, adjust, and optimize against trade-offs between project sequencing, resource allocation, and portfolio value.
- *Recommend*: Develop a final set of project prioritization recommendations for desired future state.

In summary, portfolio optimization delivers significant strategic benefits to any organization, but getting the right processes in place to collect good data is not easy. Having the right data can enable your organization to know what is happening to the portfolio (descriptive analysis), what could happen (predictive analysis), and what senior leaders should do (prescriptive analysis).

Portfolio Reports: Portfolio Bubble Charts

A bubble chart is a type of chart that displays three dimensions of data. Bubble charts can facilitate the understanding of social, economic, medical, and other scientific relationships. Bubble charts are useful graphs for comparing the relationships between data objects in more than two numeric-data dimensions: The X-axis data, the Y-axis data, and the other data represented by the bubble size, color, and shape.

The risk-value portfolio bubble chart represents a portfolio view of all projects and puts projects into one of four quadrants based on value and risk; this is important for identifying projects that drive overall greater value to the organization compared to other projects as well as highlight projects that should likely be screened out.

Let's see an example on Figure 5.2.

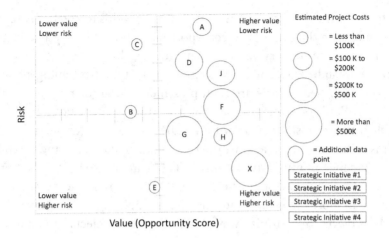

FIGURE 5.2
Risk-value portfolio bubble.

Bubble diagrams are versatile tools than can be used in multiple ways. One of them is the hierarchical format, starting on the top of the company and cascading through portfolios of different organizational levels.

Those diagrams may be used in a decentralized format, where different groups in the company construct bubble diagrams for their own projects, independently of each other.

Benefits of Portfolio Bubble Charts

One of the key benefits to a portfolio bubble chart is to quickly show the balance of the current portfolio. Using portfolio bubble charts with the portfolio governance team can focus conversations to help better manage the portfolio.

When reviewing projects that are in the higher-value or lower-risk quadrant, the portfolio governance team should ask the question, "how we can get more of these types of projects in the portfolio?" Likewise, with the lower-value or higher-risk projects, the portfolio governance team should ask how to avoid those types of projects. These discussions will greatly enhance the management of the portfolio and enable the portfolio governance team to "manage the tail" and ensure that only the best projects are selected and executed. Project reporting is a very popular capability of our commercial products adding great value and saving PM loads of time.

Your projects contain lots of data in plans, logs, registers, and also custom sources from Project, Planner, or Excel files. When you run a report, the system gets the data from your sources and uses this to create the report. Depending on the type of project reporting requested it may also include status and commentary information provided by the PM. Your report can also include properties and assurance data it has been autogenerating for you. Finished reports are then presented to you for review in either HTML, Word, or Excel format. You can then print it, save, or use the Publish option to share them with members of your project team.

It is difficult to argue against the basic value of diagrams and its ability to act as a meaningful information display. To many experts this is the reason for the popularity of bubble diagrams. The diagram indicates projects that are in more preferred quadrants, for example high importance, easy-to-do projects. In a similar way, it helps discern projects in less desired quadrants, for example low importance, difficult-to-do projects. In any case the bubble diagram is designed to act as an information display of a project portfolio, not as a decision model. Therefore, it does not contain a mechanism to help on decision-making. Bubble diagrams cannot tell what the right balance is. Management needs to decide the right balance and compare it against the actual balance. In addition, bubble diagrams do not spell out how they should be used; management needs to say how to use them, for example when to change the balance, terminate some projects, or add new ones. Bubble diagrams can be customized.

Data Needed

A prioritization scoring mechanism is typically required to build the best portfolio bubble charts (Figure 5.3).

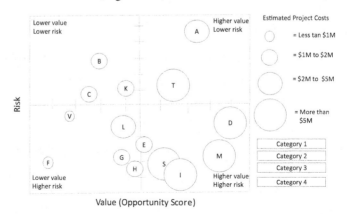

FIGURE 5.3
Example of best portfolio bubble chart.

PPM AND DECISION-MAKING

Two realities need to be taken into account about decision-making. First, it is important to recognize that decision-making is not only a business activity but a social one. It needs to be considered that human beings are involved in there. People have personal perspectives and agendas and they have many variations in capabilities. Very often a decision is made by a group of people, executed by another group, is beneficial to yet another group, and is resisted by still another group. People who belong to every group vary in their levels of experience, competence and commitment to a solution, knowledge of the facts, moral outlook, and opinions about how given decisions should be handled. Then you reach a decision that reflects the interplay of these people. Making decisions outside a social context can generate unpleasant surprises.

Second, decision makers need to recognize that decisions are the end product of dealing with constraints (knowledge, time, resources, skills, political forces, legacy, laws of nature, human laws, ethics, personalities). An effective decision process requires decision makers to surface these constraints and figure out how to craft workable decisions that accommodate them. Past personal experiences taught me that sometimes decision makers have little choice and the results of whittling generate good-enough decisions.

Just about everyone agrees that constraints can color decisions. Even strong adherents of objective decision-making grudgingly agree with this. Nevertheless, the constraints are often treated as nuisances that distract from the real decision-making effort (Davidson Frame, 2013).

By viewing projects as they would view components of an investment portfolio, managers can make decisions based not only on projected costs, but also on anticipated risks and returns in relation to other projects or initiatives. This leads to improvements in customer service and greater client loyalty.

PPM deals with the coordination and control of multiple projects pursuing the same strategic goals and competing for the same resources, whereby managers prioritize among projects to achieve strategic benefits (Cooper et al., 1997). PPM has received a stable and central position both in project management research, product development management research, and companies' management practices during the past decade. PPM has been developed into global standards (PMI, 2008) as well as practical tool books (Benko and McFarlan, 2003) that are expected to help companies organize and implement their own PPM. Companies have adopted PPM frameworks, including the use of project evaluation and decision criteria (e.g., Martinsuo, 2013), project evaluation and control routines (e.g. Müller et al., 2008), and other means to formalize their PPM (e.g., Teller et al., 2012).

Despite the variety of instructions on how projects should be selected to the portfolio, how resources should be allocated across projects, how to align the entire portfolio with strategy, and how to assess the success of the portfolio, companies still struggle with the resource sharing problem across projects (Engwall and Jerbrant, 2003) as well as constant changes in their portfolios (Elonen and Artto, 2003). It appears that, despite the PPM frameworks and their well-intended portfolio analyses and investment optimizations during portfolio planning, PPM models are critiqued (Henriksen and Traynor, 1999), attention managers give to portfolio activities is inadequate (Elonen and Artto, 2003), and working with multiple projects overloads the employees (Zika-Viktorsson et al., 2006).

Why? Among possible explanations is the lack of awareness of practice (i.e., what managers actually do) and context (i.e., what are the unique conditions in which the project portfolio is being managed). Recent empirical research indicates that many such kinds of issues may be extremely relevant to the success in PPM. For example, the resource issue raises many viewpoints of PPM in practice. On the one hand, projects need to share their resources and knowledge, diffuse good practices, and learn from each other (Nobeoka and Cusumano, 1995). Such sharing can clearly benefit the entire portfolio as capability and technology synergies can be exploited and capacity use be minimized. On the other hand, however, projects should try and enhance their autonomy to optimize their resource use in pursuing their own performance and business goals.

Focusing resources for a single project can also benefit the entire portfolio as project execution speed may be maximized and new products can be brought to market rapidly. This dilemma in resource sharing is poorly understood and hardly solved in project portfolios and is just one among others. Many other deviations from the companies' PPM frameworks appear in the day-to-day practice (e.g. Blichfeldt and Eskerod, 2008), suggesting that the current frameworks do not cover all relevant factors.

Also, the context and microlevel dynamics of portfolios generate repeated concerns for project and portfolio managers. Even if risks and uncertainties are supposed to be covered as part of portfolio analyses (e.g., Archer and Ghasemzadeh, 1999; Henriksen and Traynor, 1999), the mundane reality of new customer requests, added feature requirements, schedule and cost changes, and risk realization impact project portfolios more between portfolio analysis events than during them. This means that portfolio managers need to pay attention to their context continuously and not just during portfolio selection or other preplanned portfolio analysis events.

Changes may be necessary for optimizing the portfolio and satisfying the customers, but at the same time they alter the logic of the PPM system by displaying political and emotional decision processes instead of rational ones (e.g., Christiansen and Varnes, 2008). Implications of the context dependencies and microlevel dynamics of portfolios have not yet been sufficiently understood and explained at the portfolio level. The practice and context of PPM question the applicability of "traditional," normative decision-making centered PPM, particularly in rapidly changing business environments. Although popular press has suggested some dynamic solutions to portfolio management (Benko and McFarlan, 2003; Brown and Eisenhardt, 1998), empirical research has not yet developed or adopted feasible solutions to PPM that would sufficiently account for practice and context.

Project Portfolio Management as a Rational Decision-Making Process

PPM has become a central way for companies to manage their product development efficiently and effectively (e.g., Roussel et al., 1991). Among the key issues has been that projects are selected and managed in line with strategy and that resources are allocated to projects with the optimization of the entire portfolio in mind (e.g., Archer and Ghasemzadeh, 1999; Artto and Dietrich, 2004; Artto et al., 2004; Englund and Graham, 1999).

A lot of research attention has been placed on the tools and techniques for portfolio evaluation and prioritization (Hall and Nauda, 1990; Henriksen and Traynor, 1999; Ringuest and Graves, 1999; Spradlin and Kutoloski, 1999), portfolio-oriented product development process management (Cooper et al., 1997), and resource management dilemmas and solutions (Hansen et al., 1999; Hendriks et al., 1999; Engwall and Jerbrant, 2003). Holistic PPM frameworks have been developed (Benko and McFarlan, 2003; Dye and Pennypacker, 1999) and indicate that PPM could well be seen as an overarching system and approach for managing product development.

The frameworks and models for project selection, resource allocation, and overall portfolio management portray project choices as a rational decision-making process, which definitely has its merits. Successful firms have been shown to have a systematic approach for their portfolio evaluation, decision-making, and resource allocations (Cooper et al., 1997; Fricke and Shenhar, 2000), and some studies show clear positive associations between some systematic methods of PPM and selected measures of performance (Artto et al., 2004; Dammer and Gemünden, 2007; Fricke and Shenhar, 2000; Müller et al., 2008).

Evidence on the factors explaining PPM performance is still limited and more research is needed to test all aspects of the frameworks. With the call for more evidence, recent research is also beginning to question some of the underlying assumptions, particularly associated with viewing PPM as a rational decision process (see also Blichfeldt and Eskerod, 2008). The assumption of PPM as a rational decision process includes four underlying features that are rarely discussed but have a major impact on how PPM has been studied and executed in companies.

First, the rational approach appears to assume that projects are obedient servants that exist primarily to fulfill the strategy of the parent organization (Artto et al., 2008a). However, innovation projects are frequently used to purposefully question the strategy and are no longer necessarily limited to one company's strategic interests only (Artto et al., 2008b).

Second, project portfolio selection and management frameworks tend to assume that projects compete for the same resources and that all relevant resources are known and controlled by the company itself. Many of the optimization frameworks rely on such a premise that despite an increasing tendency of companies to collaborate with external partners in product and service development (e.g. Artto et al., 2008b), various interdependencies between projects (Nobeoka and Cusumano, 1995; Prencipe and Tell, 2001) and matrix organizations have a limited control over project resources (e.g. Perks, 2007).

Third, the rational approach appears to assume that companies are fully aware of all possible factors, both internal and external, influencing the projects. Many of the previous studies delimit their attention to the projects that are well defined and whose environments are well known, even if less well-defined projects also are being found in portfolios (Blichfeldt and

Eskerod, 2008; Loch, 2000) and many portfolio environments are inherently poorly known.

Fourth, the frameworks and related research assume that such knowledge about the projects and their execution contexts can somehow be embedded into criteria and routines that align the projects with strategy and, eventually, bring strategic benefits.

Yet, there is increasing evidence that portfolio managers are not necessarily well informed (Blichfeldt and Eskerod, 2008; Elonen and Artto, 2003) and the criteria and routines do not solve multiproject problems as expected (e.g., Engwall and Jerbrant, 2003; Zika-Viktorsson et al., 2006). As this brief overview shows, more attention needs to be paid to the assumptions associated with PPM.

Project Portfolio Management: Practice and Context

The practice of PPM in its real-life context is somewhat less rational than the decision-process-centered frameworks would suggest. This is acknowledged in some recent empirical studies that draw attention toward the day-to-day practice of portfolio management, i.e., what project and portfolio managers actually do (e.g., Blichfeldt and Eskerod, 2008; Christiansen and Varnes, 2008) besides what they should do.

Also, the dependence of the projects on their specific parent-organizational and stakeholder context as well as history (Artto et al., 2008a,b; Engwall and Jerbrant, 2003) highlights the need to examine project portfolios in their actual dynamic context, instead of assuming a stable context. Although some critical project management research has revealed various aspects of the actuality in project-based management (see e.g. Hodgson and Cicmil, 2006), they have not yet taken a holistic view of the actuality of PPM.

Increasingly, research on PPM acknowledges that different practices are needed in different contexts, following a typical contingency theory argument (e.g., Donaldson, 1987; Luthans and Stewart, 1977). Conceptual research has clearly suggested that business strategy has an influence on PPM and its success (Archer and Ghasemzadeh, 1999; Meskendahl, 2010). Increasingly, however, attention is moving from the complexities in the parent organization (see Artto et al., 2008) toward the customer needs (Voss, 2012) and uncertainties and risks in the broader business environment (Sanchez et al., 2009) as factors influencing the use and success of PPM practice.

Recent empirical studies show additional evidence of how the context of PPM appears and affects performance. Table 5.2 summarizes empirical research that raises various viewpoints to the context that have been noticed to influence either the use of PPM frameworks or its success. The key findings are discussed below. The analysis of recent empirical research

TABLE 5.2

Summary of Recent Empirical Research on PPM in Context

Reference	Data and Methodology	Key Findings	Emerging Issues and New Gaps
Biedembach and Müller, 2012	Mixed method study: interviews (18) and questionnaire (64 respondents) in pharmaceutical industry	Absorptive and adaptative capabilities are associated with PPM performance	Using external information and adjusting PPM practice based on it is relevant to success
Blomquist and Müller, 2006	Multimethod study: interviews (nine companies) and questionnaire (242 responses)	Organizational complexity explains certain portfolio management practices and middle manager's roles	Need to take into account contextual issues in selecting portfolio management practices
Dammer and Gemünden, 2007	Questionnaire study in 151 portfolios	Usefulness of project portfolio coordination mechanisms for portfolio resource allocation quality depends on the nature of the portfolio	Context dependency of portfolio management and performance
Müller et al., 2008	Questionnaire survey with 136 respondents	Various contextual factors such as dynamics, location, and governance type moderate the relationship of portfolio control and portfolio performance	Context dependency of portfolio control and performance
Olsson, 2008	Action research with a transport solutions firm	Projects in the portfolio share risks that at the portfolio level may become trends and be relevant to the business	Top managers need visibility to risk commonalities and trends in the portfolio. A risk in one project may mean opportunity for another

(Continued)

TABLE 5.2 (*Continued*)

Summary of Recent Empirical Research on PPM in Context

Reference	Data and Methodology	Key Findings	Emerging Issues and New Gaps
Perks, 2007	Qualitative embedded single case study with multiple methods in three projects of a steel manufacturing firm	Interfunctional integration is related with resource allocation and, thereby, portfolio management. Parent organization influences its portfolios through functional domination and evaluation criteria	Parent organization influences and manager's personal preferences both are relevant in PPM
Petit and Hobs, 2010: Petit 2012	Multiple case studies with four portfolios in two companies	Uncertainty and changes in the portfolio have a significant role in PPM	PPM as sensing, seizing, and transforming; PPM in dynamic environments requires further research
Teller et al., 2012	Questionnaire study with 134 firms	In complex project portfolios (where projects have interdependencies), PPM formalization is even more important than less complex	Formalization of PPM needs to take into account the context and nature of the portfolio
Unger et al., 2012	Questionnaire study with 278 respondents	PPM office may have different roles, and these roles have an influence on PPM practice	The organizational and managerial context of PPM
Zika-Viktorsson et al., 2006	Questionnaire study in nine firms	Project personnel often experiences project overload due to various multiproject issues, and this overhead has various negative consequences	Multiproject setting as a work context is relevant to how work is experienced as well as to performance.

reveals two major issues when looking at PPM in context. First, recent studies are showing evidence that the success of portfolio management indeed is dependent on the context, in line with contingency theory assumptions. Such issues as organizational complexity (Blomquist and Müller, 2006; Dammer and Gemünden, 2007; Teller et al., 2012), degree of innovativeness (Dammer and Gemünden, 2007), contextual dynamics, and organizational governance type (Müller et al., 2008), and the managerial context (Unger et al., 2012; Zika-Viktorsson et al., 2006) have been identified as relevant factors associated with either PPM practices, project portfolio success, or their relationship.

Although some of the studies look at the business or geographical context of the companies (e.g., Müller et al., 2008), attention has been directed at the parent organizational context too. For example, Perks (2007) explored how interfunctional integration in the parent organization was reflected in resource allocation choices and, thereby, portfolio management, and Dammer and Gemünden (2007) and Teller et al. (2012) looked into interdependencies among projects as a context calling for different degrees in PPM formalization.

Second, some of the studies emphasize the need to understand risks, uncertainties, and changes in the project portfolio or its context and that such dynamics should be taken into account in PPM practice. Olsson (2008) emphasized that projects in the portfolio may share risks that may become increasingly relevant business issues at the portfolio level and, therefore, need to be taken into account by managers.

Petit and Hobbs (2010) and Petit (2012) paid attention to the dynamics in the project portfolio environment and emphasized that such changes and uncertainties have a significant role for the portfolio. In fact, their study as well as some others (Biedenbach and Müller, 2012) portray PPM as a way to understand and seize external information to mold decisions and actions and, thereby, adjust the portfolio to the situation at hand. Instead of reactiveness to an upper level strategy, such evidence suggests that projects together may have more proactive strategies in their dynamic contexts, in line with recent conceptual research on project strategy (Artto et al., 2008a,b).

MAIN ROLES IN DATA ANALYTICS

Data analysis is the most in-demand skill. Granted, it's a strange one to appear on a list of the same name, but it is defined as the critical-thinking ability to interpret numbers. "It's the ability to tell a story that gives insight into a problem," says Dan Sommer, Trilogy's founder and CEO. In other words, in addition to knowing how to use specific programming languages and tools, employers need you to discern when patterns in data are meaningful, so that you can draw accurate and actionable conclusions.

Project managers must often make decisions based on partial information. This "project tunnel vision" might push projects ahead, but it does not consider the impact these tactical decisions can have on the organization as a whole.

Project tunnel vision is more than just a lack of data and limited reporting. The tunnel vision syndrome begins with the people and culture of running projects. Many project management organizations work reactively. Project leaders are assigned whatever projects are deemed most important. They are directed to focus on delivering the best possible outcome—which at the individual project level means a tactical outcome.

Strategic project management concepts are new to most organizations, and many of them are not prepared to move to a strategic mindset. This shift can only begin by first evaluating their current state of affairs and developing a plan of action to take projects to the next level.

Turning project management into a strategic asset means including analytics in PPM and governance frameworks. Business performance management (BPM) technologies and methodologies can help.

BPM is a discipline that grew out of the business intelligence world. BPM allows companies to mine business data from various sources, analyze it, and take appropriate action. By continuously reviewing dashboards, BPM delivers strategic information businesses need to balance specific business activities against predefined goals. BPM enables companies to identify problem areas quickly and forecast results more accurately. BPM is also used for risk analysis and to conduct what-if scenarios to improve future performance.

Although BPM is commonly used in areas such as operational performance, sales performance, and financial performance, the project management world has not used it consistently. The concept of a balanced scorecard is an excellent example of a BPM methodology often not employed by project management groups.

Balanced scorecards have been at the center of the BPM world since its beginnings. They incorporate financial and nonfinancial metrics to monitor performance against specific targets. In addition, methodologies such as activity-based costing (ABC), also popularized by BPM, can provide excellent insight into projects by assigning cost values to all activities and resources impacting projects and their stakeholders. These BPM methodologies are commonly employed by businesses to make strategic decisions and ensure that projects are performing to expectations.

Based on that, to develop a solid performance management and analytics strategy, project management professionals need to ask themselves the following questions:

- How easily accessible is project data? Is data siloed or centralized?
- What are the primary components that need to be assessed across all projects? Is it resource driven? Is it budget driven?
- What are their organizations' goals and targets? How will they be measured? Do they have defined key performance indicators (KPIs) in place?
- What is their risk management strategy? What kind of tools do they have in place to conduct what-if analysis?

A well-thought-out governance framework and a PPM strategy is the first step in identifying what metrics and analytics are needed to improve project performance. PPM means mining the mission-critical project data captured throughout your organization and measuring it against corporate goals and KPIs. Although many models of measurement are available, the biggest challenge lies in quickly accessing the data from multiple sources, processing the information, and then providing results to the appropriate decision makers. Consequently, true project analytics means that organizations need to respond to their project information with the same conviction and care as their colleagues are currently doing in sales, operations, and finance.

Role

The senior PPM analyst is responsible for data management, analysis, and reporting for the CIO organization. This position will be responsible for providing and presenting strategic and actionable reporting for various target audiences, utilizing PPM and reporting tools. In addition, this position will develop and implement process automation and improvement and will frequently provide periodic and recurring reporting for executive management, which may be presented to the senior operating committee.

Responsibilities

- Provide ad hoc reporting to management to mitigate risk and drive business decisions
- Responsible for delivering actionable business intelligence while maintaining reporting to leadership of required metrics

- Analyze and interpret data regarding key performance metrics for various target audiences
- Identify opportunities for process improvement
- Strong critical thinking skills to scope and frame data and analytics challenges
- Strong communication abilities to uncover core analytical issues and propose and implement efficient solutions
- Present data to all levels within the organization
- Take ownership and accountability for systematic, project, or data-related issues to drive delivery from cross-functional teams

Requirements

- Strong consulting skills to build strong relationships with analytics teams and technology partners to effectively understand and support analytics needs
- Effective presentation skills to train and support analytics partners
- Some tools experience
- Ability to communicate with and present to all levels of management
- Anticipate business needs, organize, and prioritize to ensure the success of multiple stakeholders
- Strong quantitative/analytical background, and 3+ years of data analysis experience

DATA ANALYTICS AND PROJECT PORTFOLIO PERFORMANCE

Worldwide revenues for big data and business analytics are expected to grow to more than $187 billion by 2019 and the project management industry is projected to hit $5.81 trillion by 2020. Here are how some organizations are leveraging data analytics to improve their project performance (Gartner group).

Gartner predicts that the following four trends will drive fundamental changes in the use of data and analytics:

- Instead of just reflecting business performance, data analytics will become the driver of operations.

- Data and analytics will become infused in an organization's architecture from end to end, creating a holistic approach and this will include strategic project management in enterprise program management offices (EPMOs).
- Executives will use data and analytics for business strategy and growth, creating new additional roles for professionals.
- Experts share insights on how data improves project performance.

Companies of all sizes have been using data analytics to seek out opportunities, reduce costs, create efficiencies, make better and faster decisions, and ultimately increase customer satisfaction; this also translates at the project, program, and portfolio levels since these greatly enable company-wide strategy.

At the Chicago Bulls, Matthew Kobe, director of analytics, says its business strategy and analytics team uses consumer insights to drive the strategic direction of the organization. They use data analytics to focus on three key areas of insight—fan levels, business transactions, and digital engagement—to inform the organization's strategic choices. He shares more about their focus on the three areas below:

1. *Fan level insights*: The Bulls are building a robust CRM and data warehouse solution that delivers a more holistic view of our fans. "We seek to understand psychographic elements that help us to understand why a person is engaging and transacting with the Bulls," says Matthew. They also want to "understand satisfaction and areas for improvement by capturing fan specific feedback on all elements of the fan experience."
2. *Transactional insights*: The team analyzes all business transactions including ticketing, concessions, and merchandise, and wherever possible, Matthew says "We tie these transactional elements back to the fan to build out a more complete customer view."
3. *Digital engagement insights*: "The Bulls have a significant digital presence illustrated by the second largest social media following for any sports team in North America," says Kobe. Because of this, they work to understand the types of content fans are engaging with and how those engagements drive their fans downstream behaviors. They again make every effort to link engagements back to the fan to help their continued effort to further expand on their customer view.

"With these three areas under our purview, we are able to more effectively influence change across the organization. Specifically, we have impacted nearly every area that influences a fan's experience with the Bulls: Ticketing, Sponsorship, Digital Content, Marketing, and Concessions," he says.

Jason Levin, vice president of Institutional Research at Western Governors University (WGU), also shared how they use data analytics to create project wins. "Conceptually, the most important data for project success is having a measurement plan that includes implementation fidelity and efficacy," he says.

He suggests answering this question: "How do we know we are doing what we intended to do?" and "How do we know if what we did worked?" Jason elaborates further on their methods for measuring implementation fidelity and efficacy.

For implementation fidelity, WGU has used many methods, ranging from analyzing log data of student sessions with electronic learning materials to having faculty use hashtag notations in the student notes.

For efficacy, "our bias is to use randomized control trials, but we also use quasi-experimental methods. The most important data is to have a clearly defined outcome variable that can be reliably measured. Western Governors University (WGU) has a competitive advantage with outcome variables compared to traditional higher education institutions. At WGU, all our assessments are centrally developed to rigorous standards. This system of assessment produces much more reliable data than having faculty individually assigning letter grades."

He also describes another unique aspect of data at WGU: its "domain taxonomy or hierarchy of learning outcomes mapped to learning materials and assessments. Student learning behavior can be mapped between the electronic course materials and assessment. Formative assessment data is more predictive of success on the high stakes assessment than simple pageviews."

To make the best decisions, companies need to be able to extract precise and relevant information from the data available. Absent this, raw data, no matter the quantity, serves no purpose. Ultimately, companies are seeking the type of information that tells them what their customers want most and is critical for guidance on project initiatives, direction, execution, and metrics.

CONCLUSIONS

In current global markets, as a result of the recent economic turmoil, organizations are placed under further pressure to do more with less. This suggests that there is a greater need to utilize scarce resources optimally in order to achieve the organization's strategic intent. PPM is the function in the organization that will help to achieve this if it is positioned and used correctly.

To conclude

- Data analytics initiatives may help businesses increase revenues, improve operational efficiency, optimize marketing campaigns and customer service efforts, respond more quickly to emerging market trends, feel safer as organization, and gain a competitive advantage over rivals. For each particular application, the data that's analyzed can consist of either historical records or new information that has been processed for real-time analytics uses.

  Three levels of data analysis can be distinguished: descriptive analysis, predictive analysis, and prescriptive analysis. In summary, portfolio optimization delivers significant strategic benefits to any organization, but getting the right processes in place to collect good data is not easy. Having the right data can enable your organization to know what is happening to the portfolio (descriptive analysis), what could happen (predictive analysis) and what senior leaders should do (prescriptive analysis).
- One of the key benefits of a portfolio report (it may be a portfolio bubble chart) is to quickly show the balance of the current portfolio. Using portfolio bubble charts with the portfolio governance team can focus conversations to help better manage the portfolio.
- Second, decision makers need to recognize that decisions are the end product of dealing with constraints (knowledge, time, resources, skills, political forces, legacy, laws of nature, human laws, ethics, personalities). An effective decision process requires decision makers to surface these constraints and figure out how to craft workable decisions that accommodate them.
- The practice and context of PPM question the applicability of "traditional," normative decision-making-centered PPM, particularly in rapidly changing business environments. The practice of PPM in its

real-life context is somewhat less rational than the decision-process-centered frameworks would suggest.

- The senior PPM analyst is responsible for data management, analysis, and reporting for the CIO organization. Project managers must often make decisions based on partial information.

It can be argued that, despite the focus of investment on tactical problems as opposed to achieving strategic objectives, organizations are still successful. However, organizations may be successful for other reasons, such as having a unique product offering, service, or presence in the market. Nevertheless, one respondent reported that their organization achieved increasing success since adopting a portfolio management approach and achieving better alignment of initiatives with strategic objectives.

REFERENCES

Archer, N., & Ghasemzadeh, F. (1999). Project portfolio selection techniques: A review and a suggested integrated approach. In: Dye, L.D. & Pennypacker, J.S. (Eds.), *Project Portfolio Management. Selecting and Prioritizing Projects for Competitive Advantage.* Center for Business Practices, USA, pp. 207–238.

Artto, K.A., & Dietrich, P.H. (2004). Strategic business management through multiple projects. In: Morris, P.W.G. & Pinto, J.K. (Eds.), *The Wiley Guide to Managing Projects.* London: Wiley, pp. 144–176.

Artto, K., Kujala, J., Dietrich, P., & Martinsuo, M. (2008a). What is project strategy? *International Journal of Project Management* 26 (1), 4–12.

Artto, K., Martinsuo, M., Dietrich, P., & Kujala, J. (2008b). Project strategy – strategy types and their contents in innovation projects. International HYPERLINK "https://www.researchgate.net/journal/1753-8378_International_Journal_of_Managing_Projects_in_Business" *International Journal of Managing Projects in Business* 1 (1), 49–70.

Biedenbach, T., & Müller, R. (2012). Absorptive, innovative and adaptive capabilities and their impact on project and project portfolio performance. *International Journal of Project Management* 30 (5), 621–635.

Blichfeldt, B.S., & Eskerod, P. (2008). Project portfolio management – There's more to it than what management enacts. *International Journal of Project Management* 26, 357–365

Blomquist, T., & Müller, R. (2006). Practices, roles, and responsibilities of middle managers in program and portfolio management. *Project Management Journal* 37 (1), 52–66.

Brown, S.L., & Eisenhardt, K.M. (1998). *Competing on the Edge: Strategy as Structured Chaos. Boston,* MA: Harvard Business School Press.

Christiansen, J.K. & Varnes, C. (2008). From models to practice: decision making at portfolio meetings. *International Journal of Quality and Reliability Management* 25 (1), 87–101.

Dammer, H. & Gemünden, H.G. (2007). Improving resource allocation quality in multi-project environments: evaluating the effects of coordination mechanisms. Paper presented at EURAM European Academy of Management Conference, Paris, France (16–19 May, 2007).

Davidson Frame J. (2012). *Framing Decisions: Decision-Making that Accounts for Irrationality, People and Constraints*. San Francisco: Wiley and Sons.

Donaldson, L. (1987). Strategy and structural adjustment and regain fit to performance: in defence of contingency theory. *Journal of Management Studies* 24 (1), 1–24.

Dye, L. & Pennypacker, J. (Eds.), 1999. *Project Portfolio Management. Selecting and Prioritizing Projects for Competitive Advantage*. Center for Business Practices, USA.

Englund, R.L. & Graham, R.J. (1999), From experience: linking projects to strategy. *Journal of Product Innovation Management* 16 (1), 52–64.

Engwall, M. & Jerbrant, A. (2003). The resource allocation syndrome: the prime challenge of multi-project management? *International Journal of Project Management* 21 (6), 403–409.

Fricke, S.E. and Shenhar, A.J. (2000), Managing multiple engineering projects in a manufacturing support environment, *IEEE Transactions on Engineering Management* 47 (2), 258–268.

Hall, D.L. & Nauda, A. (1990). An interactive approach for selecting IR&D projects. *IEEE Transactions on Engineering Management* 37, 126–133.

Hansen, M.T. (1999). The search-transfer problem: the role of weak ties in sharing knowledge across organization subunits. *Administrative Science Quarterly* 44, 82–111.

Hendriks, M.H.A., Voeten, B., & Kroep, L. (1999). Human resource allocation in a multi-project R&D environment. Resource capacity allocation and project portfolio planning in practice. *International Journal of Project Management* 17 (3), 181–188.

Henriksen, A. & Traynor, A. (1999). A practical R&D project-selection scoring tool. *IEEE Transactions on Engineering Management* 46 (2), 158–170.

Hodgson, D., Cicmil, S. (Eds.), 2006. *Making Projects Critical*. Palgrave MacMillan, USA.

Loch, C. (2000). Tailoring product development to strategy: case of a European technology manufacturer. *European Management Journal* 18 (3), 246–258.

Luthans, F., Stewart, T.I., 1977. A general contingency theory of management. *Academy of Management Review* 2 (2), 181–195.

Martinsuo, M. (2013). Project portfolio management in practice and in context. *International Journal of Project Management*, Elsevier.

Meskendahl ,(2010).The influence of business strategy on project portfolio management and its success—A conceptual framework.

Müller, R., Martinsuo, M., & Blomquist, T. (2008). Project portfolio control and portfolio management performance in different contexts. *Project Management Journal* 39 (3), 28–42.

Nobeoka, K. & Cusumano, M.A., 1995. Multiproject strategy, design transfer, and project performance: a survey of automobile development projects in the US and Japan. *IEEE Transactions on Engineering Management* 42 (4), 397–409.

Olsson, R., 2008. Risk management in a multi-project environment: an approach to manage portfolio risks. *International Journal of Quality & Reliability Management* 25 (1), 60–71.

Perks, H. (2007). Inter-functional integration and industrial new product portfolio decision making: exploring and articulating the linkages. *Creativity and Innovation Management* 16 (2), 152–164.

Petit, Y. (2012). Project portfolios in dynamic environments: organizing for uncertainty. *International Journal of Project Management* 30 (5), 539–553.

Petit, Y., Hobbs, B. (2010). Project portfolios in dynamic environments: sources of uncertainty and sensing mechanisms. *Project Management Journal* 41 (4), 46–58.

Prencipe, A. & Tell, F. (2001), Inter-project learning: processes and outcomes of knowledge codification in project-based firms, *Research Policy* 30 (9), 1373–1394.

Project Management Institute. (2008). *A Guide to the Project Management Body of Knowledge (PMBOK® guide)*—Fourth edition. Newtown Square, PA: Project Management Institute.

Ringuest, J. & Graves, S. (1999). Formulating R&D portfolios that account for risk. *Research Technology Management* 42 (6), 40–43.

Roussel, P.A., Saad, K.N., & Erickson, T.J. (1991). *Third Generation R&D: Managing the Link to Corporate Strategy.* Boston, MA: Arthur D. Little, Inc.

Sanchez, H., Robert, B., Bourgault, M. & Pellerin, R. (2009). Risk management applied to projects, programs, and portfolios. *International Journal of Managing Projects* in Business 2 (1), 14–35.

Spradlin, C. & Kutoloski, D., 1999. Action-oriented portfolio management. *Research Technology Management* 42 (2), 26–32.

Teller, J., Unger, B., Kock, A., & Gemünden, H.G. (2012). Formalization of project portfolio management: the moderating role of project portfolio complexity. *International Journal of Project Management* 30 (5), 596–607.

Unger, B.N., Kock, A., Gemünden, H.G., & Jonas, D. (2012). Enforcing strategic fit of project portfolios by project termination: an empirical study on senior management involvement. *International Journal of Project Management* 30 (6), 675–685.

Voss, M. (2012). Impact of customer integration on project portfolio management and its success—Developing a conceptual framework.

Zika-Viktorsson, A., Sundström, P., & Engwall, M. (2006). Project overload: an exploratory study of work and management in multi-project settings. *International Journal of Project Management* 24 (5), 385–394.

6

Earned Value Method

Werner Meyer

CONTENTS

INTRODUCTION

The well-known management consultant Peter Drucker (1909–2005) once said: "If you can't measure it, you can't manage it." Most project managers know this very well and project teams are often obsessed with finding better ways to measure project performance. Projects generate large amounts of data and there is usually no shortage of methods to report project performance. The challenge is, however, that selective performance reporting may hide inherent problems from decision makers until it is too late to save the project. The earned value management (EVM) method gives practitioners a clear, numerical method for measuring project performance, and it allows managers to ask critical questions about the actual progress of a project. In this chapter, the principles of EVM and some common pitfalls are discussed.

EVM METHODS

In the late 1800s, techniques similar to the basic EVM methods were used to report work and cost performance in factories in the United States. During the 1960s, the U.S. Air Force issued the cost/schedule control systems criteria (C/SCSC), outlining 35 criteria to be met by private contractors wishing to use EVM on government projects. These criteria were refined by the U.S. Department of Defense and in 1998, the ANSI-EIA 748 Guide for EVM was officially published for public use (TechAmerica, 2013). Today, EVM is part of all the well-known project management standards and is widely used by project practitioners. Readers interested in the history of EVM are referred to Fleming and Koppelman (2010) for a detailed account.

The primary aim of EVM is to use a consistent method of project progress measurement based on the actual work completed. EVM methods can be categorized as either descriptive or predictive. Descriptive EVM methods use past project performance to report how well the project is performing. Predictive EVM methods are used to forecast the expected future performance of the project. EVM methods are best described with an example.

Figure 6.1 shows the timeline of a simple project: to build a wooden deck. The project has three tasks: design the deck, build the deck, and paint the

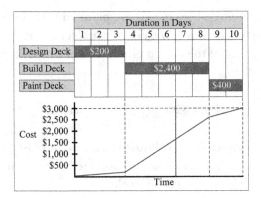

FIGURE 6.1
Deck project.

deck. The estimated cost of each task is shown in the bar representing the task, and a graph with the cumulative cost of the project is shown below the timeline. The owner of the deck decided to use a different contractor for each activity. The design and paint costs are fixed and include material and equipment. The cost of the "Build Deck" task has an hourly rate of $60 (daily rate of $480) and the owner supplies all the material to the contractor, free of charge. To simplify the example, it is assumed that the costs are spread linearly over the duration of each task and that the contractors will work over weekends.

Descriptive EVM

It is clear from the diagram that the total planned project cost is $3,000 and the total planned duration is 10 days. In EVM terminology, the total planned cost is known as the *budget at completion* (BAC).

The project starts on time and the design contractor completes the design work at the end of day 3 and invoices the client for $200. The deck building starts on the morning of day 4. At the end of day 6 (indicated with a solid vertical line at the end of day 6 in Figure 6.1), the owner calls a meeting with the building contractor to assess the progress. The building contractor reports that the work is 70% complete, and a quick measurement of the deck area by the owner confirms this. At the meeting, the building contractor also gives the owner the first invoice for the work done so far. The invoice amount is $1,750, and the contractor explains that they had to work additional hours in the previous few days. The owner accepts the invoice, mindful of the fact that very good progress has been made.

In EVM terminology, the cumulative planned cost at the status date is known as the *planned value* (PV). For this project, the PV at the end of day 6 is the planned cost of the design plus 3 days at the building daily rate of $480:

$$PV = \$200 + (3 \times \$480) = \$1,640$$

The cumulative invoiced cost is known as the *actual cost* (AC). At the end of day 6, the owner has received and accepted invoices for $200 for the design and $1,750 for the building work:

$$AC = \$200 + \$1,750 = \$1,950$$

The measured completed work is now converted to a monetary value, which is known as the *earned value* (EV). The contractor reported that 70% of the work has been completed, so the EV for the project is $200 for the design, which is 100% complete, plus the completed work for the deck:

$$EV = (100\% \times \$200) + (70\% \times \$2,400) = \$1,880$$

The EV represents the value of completed work according to the original plan.

These three parameters, PV, AC, and EV, form the basis of all the EVM calculations. This may seem quite simple, but it will later be shown that the measurement of completed work to determine the EV can be difficult and, at times, very subjective.

With the three EVM parameters established, the status of this project can now be explored. First, we are interested in determining whether the project is deviating from its plan in terms of time and cost. The following variance calculations are used for this:

$$\text{Cost variance} = CV = EV - AC \qquad (6.1)$$

$$CV\% = \frac{CV}{EV} \times 100 \qquad (6.2)$$

$$\text{Schedule variance} = SV = EV - PV \qquad (6.3)$$

$$SV\% = \frac{SV}{PV} \qquad (6.4)$$

For our example, we have CV = $1,880 − $1,950 = − $70 and

$$CV\% = \frac{-\$70}{\$1,880} \times 100 = -3.7\%$$

These values are negative and indicate that the project is overspent by $70 or 3.7%. We also have SV = $1,880 − $1,640 = $240 and

$$SV\% = \frac{\$240}{\$1,640} \times 100 = 14.6\%$$

These values are positive and indicate that the project is ahead of schedule by 14.6%. Presenting the schedule variance in monetary terms may be counterintuitive since the SV shows that we are $240 ahead of schedule but, for some of the calculations that follow, we have to work with the same unit of measurement, which makes this approach useful.

The project's time and cost performance can also be communicated as an index. For cost, we have the cost performance index (CPI) and for the schedule, we have the schedule performance index (SPI):

$$CPI = \frac{EV}{AC} \tag{6.5}$$

$$SPI = \frac{EV}{PV} \tag{6.6}$$

For the CPI, the EV is compared to the AC, which means that we determine how efficiently the available money is being used. For the SPI, the EV is compared to the PV, which is a comparison of the actual and expected value added over the same period. SPI is thus an indicator of how efficiently we are using the available time. For our example, we have the following results:

$$CPI = \frac{\$1,880}{\$1,950} = 0.96$$

$$SPI = \frac{\$1,880}{\$1,640} = 1.15$$

When EV < AC, the cost of adding project value is higher than planned and the CPI is less than 1. When EV < PV, the project is producing its planned deliverables more slowly than planned and the SPI is less than 1. As general rule, CPI < 1 indicates overspending, CPI > 1 indicates underspending, and CPI = 1 indicates spending exactly as planned. When SPI < 1, the project is behind schedule, when SPI > 1, it is ahead of schedule, and when SPI = 1, it is exactly on schedule.

From these calculations, it is clear that EVM is concerned with the actual measurable progress made on the project, and not the elapsed time. On most projects, it is unlikely that the physical percentage of work complete will be the same as the elapsed time, unless it is a very simple project. The percentage of schedule complete at the status date is calculated as:

$$\text{Schedule}\,\%\,\text{complete} = \frac{\text{status date} - \text{start date}}{\text{end date} - \text{start date}} \times 100 \qquad (6.7)$$

For the sample project, this is:

$$\text{Schedule}\,\%\,\text{complete} = \frac{\text{day}\,6 - \text{day}\,0}{\text{day}\,10 - \text{day}\,0} \times 100\% = 60\%$$

The planned percentage of work complete at the status date, also known as the baseline percentage complete, is calculated from the PV and the BAC:

$$\text{Baseline}\,\%\,\text{complete} = \frac{\text{PV}}{\text{BAC}} \times 100 \qquad (6.8)$$

For the sample project, this is:

$$\text{Baseline}\,\%\,\text{complete} = \frac{\$1,640}{\$3,000} \times 100 = 54.7\%$$

The actual percentage of work completed for the project is:

$$\%\,\text{work complete} = \frac{\text{EV}}{\text{BAC}} \times 100 \qquad (6.9)$$

For the sample project, this is:

$$\%\,\text{work complete} = \frac{\$1,880}{\$3,000} \times 100 = 62.7\%$$

Comparing the percentage of work complete to the baseline percentage complete confirms that the project is ahead of schedule.

Equations 6.1–6.9 cover the EVM assessment of a project at a selected status date. In the next section, methods for forecasting the project's future performance are discussed.

Predictive EVM

Predictive EVM uses past performance to forecast the future performance of a project. Three parameters are used in EVM forecasting: cost, time, and the cost performance required to meet a target project cost. The forecast of a project's total cost is known as the estimate at completion (EAC) and is based on the actual cost to date (AC) plus the cost required to complete the project, a.k.a. the estimate to complete (ETC).

$$EAC = AC + ETC \qquad (6.10)$$

The AC is fixed at the status date, but different methods are used to calculate the ETC based on assumptions about the past and future performance of the project. These assumptions are the following:

a. Past performance was exceptional and the project will proceed as per the original plan.
b. Past performance will continue in the future.
c. Future performance is a function of the past cost and time performance.

If we hold the optimistic view that past performance was an exception and the project will proceed as per the original plan, we have:

$$EAC_{optimistic} = AC + (BAC - EV) \qquad (6.11)$$

The ETC is simply the value that still has to be added after the status date. This parameter is also known as the optimistic EAC. For our sample project, this is EAC = $1,950 + ($3,000 − $1,880) = $3,070. Note that the project's cost at completion is expected to overrun by the CV amount.

If we assume that the past cost performance, indicated by the CPI, will continue into the future, we have:

$$EAC_{realistic} = AC + \left(\frac{BAC - EV}{CPI} \right) \qquad (6.12)$$

The ETC is the remaining value to be added divided by the CPI to adjust for the cost performance. This is also known as the realistic EAC. For our sample project, this is EAC = $1,950 + ($3,000 − $1,880)/0.96 = $3,112.

If we assume that the past performance is a function of both the cost and time performance, we have:

$$EAC_{\text{best practices}} = AC + \left(\frac{BAC - EV}{CPI \times SPI} \right) \qquad (6.13)$$

The ETC is the remaining value to be added divided by the product of the CPI and SPI to adjust for time and cost performance. This method is sometimes referred to as the best practices ETC. For our sample project, this is: EAC = $1,950 + ($3,000 − $1,880)/(0.96 × 1.15) = $2,963. For the sample project, this result is unlikely since it is less than the BAC. This highlights the importance of understanding and motivating the assumptions that are made when an EAC method is selected.

A variation on the EAC method is the recent trend EAC. With this method, it is assumed that the CPI over a specific time period is an indicator of future performance, and the remaining value to be added is divided by the CPI for the indicated period.

$$EAC_{\text{recent trend}} = AC + \frac{(BAC - EV)}{\left(\sum_{i=1}^{n} EV_i \right) \bigg/ \left(\sum_{i=1}^{n} AC_i \right)} \qquad (6.14)$$

The denominator term is the cumulative EV divided by the cumulative AC over the n periods that are considered to give the representative CPI.

The expected variance at completion (VAC) for the project is the difference between the baseline budget (BAC) and the EAC:

$$VAC = BAC - EAC \qquad (6.15)$$

For the sample project, using the realistic EAC, this is: VAC = $3,000 − $3,112 = −$112, which is an overrun of $112. A positive result would indicate a budget underrun.

The to complete performance index (TCPI) is the CPI that must be achieved to meet a specific target EAC. TCPI is calculated by dividing the value of the remaining work by the available budget of the project. The first approach is to calculate the TCPI to achieve the project's original planned budget:

$$\text{TCPI}_{\text{BAC}} = \frac{(\text{BAC} - \text{EV})}{(\text{BAC} - \text{AC})} \tag{6.16}$$

For the sample project, this is $\text{TCPI}_{\text{BAC}} = \dfrac{(\$3{,}000 - \$1{,}880)}{(\$3{,}000 - \$1{,}950)} = 1.07$. The second approach is to calculate the TCPI to achieve a reestimated EAC. The reestimated EAC could be from one of the calculations above or physically reestimating the remaining work on the project.

$$\text{TCPI}_{\text{EAC}} = \frac{(\text{BAC} - \text{EV})}{(\text{EAC} - \text{AC})} \tag{6.17}$$

The time estimate at completion (TEAC) of a project cannot be calculated in the same way as the cost since, unlike cost, unused time does not accumulate. Two methods are used to calculate TEAC, and it should be noted; these methods are broad estimates of the time to complete. The first approach is based on the assumption that past performance will continue into the future. The TEAC is calculated by dividing the total project duration by the SPI. This method assumes that the SPI will remain constant throughout the life of the project.

$$\text{TEAC}_{\text{realistic}} = \frac{\text{end date} - \text{start date}}{\text{SPI}} \tag{6.18}$$

For this sample project, this is $\text{TEAC}_{\text{realistic}} = 10/1.15 = 8.7\,\text{days}$. A second, more optimistic, approach assumes that past performance was exceptional and the remainder of the project will proceed as planned. This approach assumes that the TEAC will be the original schedule at completion (SAC) minus the time variance (TV).

$$\text{TEAC}_{\text{optimistic}} = \text{SAC} - \text{TV} \tag{6.19}$$

The time variance is calculated from PV rate per time unit:

$$\text{TV} = \frac{\text{SV}}{\text{PV rate}} \tag{6.20}$$

The PV rate is the average budgeted cost per time unit of the project. The same time unit must be used for all the calculations (e.g., hours, days, and weeks).

$$PV\,rate = \frac{BAC}{SAC} \qquad (6.21)$$

Applying these formulae to the sample project, we have:

$$SV = \$240$$

$$PV\ rate = \frac{BAC}{SAC} = \frac{\$3,000}{10\ days} = \$300$$

$$TV = \frac{SV}{PV\ rate} = \frac{\$240}{\$300} = 0.8$$

$$TEAC_{optimistic} = 10 - 0.8 = 9.2\ days$$

From these calculations, it is predicted that the project will finish on the morning of the 10th day, which is slightly earlier than originally planned. This result is consistent with the SPI result, which indicates that the project is ahead of schedule.

A third method known as earned schedule provides more accurate estimates of the project TEAC. For a detailed explanation of earned schedule, readers are referred to Lipke (2009).

EARNED VALUE GRAPHS

The sample project used in this chapter is very simple and has only three work packages. On large projects, there could be hundreds of work packages. Plotting project cost and time data for multiple work packages on a graph is useful since it shows how the EVM variables behave over time.

The cost of a project is closely linked to the work or effort that is planned for the project. Project effort is typically low at the start of the project, then picks up as the project is executed, and tapers off toward the end. A graph of the cumulative effort over time will produce an S-curve and, since the cost is linked to the effort, a graph of the cumulative cost, or PV, follows the same curve. This behavior is illustrated in Figure 6.2. The *BAC* is the maximum *PV* value at the end of the project. Note that the *BAC* of $1,000 was chosen arbitrarily for the purpose of illustration.

The S-curve is also known as the performance measurement baseline (PMB) for the project. Plotting the actual performance of the project at

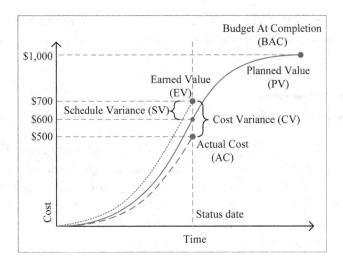

FIGURE 6.2
Cumulative PV, EV, and AC plot.

regular time intervals gives a visual representation of the EV and AC trends (Figure 6.2). Note that the values for EV and AC were chosen arbitrarily for the purpose of explaining the concept.

INTERPRETING EARNED VALUE RESULTS

The results from the EVM calculations should be interpreted with care since obvious cost and time over- or underruns may be misleading. In our sample project, we have SPI = 1.15, which indicates that the project is ahead of schedule, and we have CPI = 0.96, which indicates that the project is overspending. This appears to be favorable in terms of time but less favorable in terms of cost. However, if the client has funding constraints, this situation may lead to the project not being completed at all. Projects that must meet specific time deadlines, such as the Olympic Games, may be willing to spend a bit more money to achieve their end date. Interpretation of EVM results should, therefore, be done in the context of the project objectives defined in the project charter or the project business case.

The second problem with the interpretation of EVM results is that calculations based on the entire project may hide problems in the details.

We will later see that a favorable SPI (>1) may hide underlying problems and that the project may overrun its schedule even if the SPI is greater than 1.

SETTING UP FOR EVM

Successful EVM is only possible if a project is specifically planned to use EVM. Trying to implement EVM as an afterthought is seldom successful since cost and schedule information may not be correctly aligned, and the required progress measurement methods may not be possible. Planning for EVM should address the project scope, work breakdown structure, control accounts, and measurement methods.

Project Scope

Effective EVM requires complete definition of the scope of work. If the scope of work is incomplete, scope changes are bound to arise during the project's execution, which makes the forecasts from EVM calculations unreliable.

Work Breakdown Structure (WBS)

The WBS is a major input for the development of project cost and time estimates. If the WBS is not well-defined the details of deliverable and task variations may be hidden, which limits the project team's ability to take effective corrective action.

Control Accounts

Control accounts are selected deliverables or work packages where lower-level planned and actual performance data are consolidated. Control accounts are created since it is not always viable to plan and track actual costs and progress at the lowest level of the WBS. The definition of control accounts should consider the level and type of reporting that is required for the project. When building a house, for example, the owner is not interested in how many bricks are laid and how much cement is used when the walls are built. The owner is only interested in the total progress of the walls. The building contractor may, however, be interested in the details and may set up lower-level control accounts to measure progress.

Progress Measurement Methods

The most important aspect of planning for EVM is defining the progress measurement methods that will be used. There are six measurement methods that are commonly used. These methods are also referred to as rules of credit.

UNITS COMPLETED

The units completed method is the most accurate form of measuring progress. With this method, the physical progress is measured in the planned units of work (e.g., meters completed, number of network points installed, and square meters painted). The measured units can easily be converted to a percentage using the following formula:

$$\% \text{completed} = \frac{\text{actual units}}{\text{planned units}} \times 100 \qquad (6.22)$$

Units completed is most often used when the project manager is in direct control of the work performed. Units completed is, however, not always a suitable method for measurement. In software, for example, there is no generally accepted unit of progress measurement, and even if a unit is defined, such as lines of code, it would be difficult to estimate the number of lines required when the project is planned.

INCREMENTAL MILESTONES

The incremental milestones (a.k.a. weighted milestones) method is used where the project manager is not in direct control of the detailed work performed but is interested in the overall progress of the project.

With this method, the project stakeholders determine significant measurement milestones during project planning and agree on the percentage progress each milestone adds to the project. This method is often used when work is contracted to one or more subcontractors. Progress payments equal to the percentage progress are sometimes made when the agreed milestones are achieved, but the payment amounts do not have to match the milestone percentages and could be agreed upon separately.

START/FINISH METHOD

The start/finish method (a.k.a. the fixed formula method) is used when the progress made is difficult to determine but the start and finish are clear. With this method, it is agreed that a certain percentage of progress is allocated when the task starts, and the remainder is allocated when the task is completed. Typical percentages splits are 0/100, 25/75, and 50/50.

This method is not suitable for tasks or work packages with very long durations and is often used for tasks that are shorter than 2 weeks. Progress payments may be linked to the agreed percentages.

SUPERVISOR/RESOURCE ESTIMATE

This method is used when the progress made is difficult to measure but the people performing the work (or their supervisors) can give a fair estimate of the progress made based on their experience. This technique is often used by knowledge workers such as software developers, researchers, and designers. The initial estimate is made in terms of time or effort required to perform the task, and the percentage of progress reflects the resource or supervisor's assessment of the progress made.

COST RATIO

The cost ratio method is used when there is a strong correlation between the money spent on doing a task and the progress made on the task. The money spent is then used as an indicator of the progress. This method can be used for work that comprises different activities, equipment, material, etc.

but hides the complexity of measuring the progress for each of the items that make up the cost.

The cost ratio method requires well-planned work and accurate cost estimates. The risk of this method is that all the money could be used, indicating 100% completion; yet the work is not done. This method often has retention and performance clauses in the contract.

WEIGHTED OR EQUIVALENT UNITS

The weighted or equivalent units method is used when the final deliverable comprises many components that are measured in different units, but the entire project or deliverable is measured using a single measurement unit (e.g., volume of concrete, tons of steel, and meters of pipeline)

Example: A company is building a new warehouse that measures 1,000 m². They appoint a primary contractor to manage the subcontractors and to report on the progress of the building. Reporting progress on each element of work creates a confusing report, which is difficult to explain and interpret in terms of the overall progress. The project manager agrees with the owner that equivalent units measurement in the form of square meters completed will be used.

Table 6.1 shows how the units for the project are set up. The Allowed Credit for each subtask is allocated by the contractor based on the value or effort involved. The Total Units are the estimated quantities for the project. The Credit Quantity is the product of the Allowed Credit and the Total Units. The Credit m² is the proportion of the Credit Quantity multiplied by the total area of the building. For the earthworks, this is:

$$\text{Credit m}^2 = \frac{\text{earthworks credit quantity}}{\text{Total credit quantity}} \times 1,000 \text{ m}^2 = \frac{90}{520.96} = 172.76 \text{ m}^2$$

The Earned m² is calculated from the Units to Date. For roofing, this is:

$$\text{Earned m}^2 = \frac{\text{units to date}}{\text{Total units}} \times \text{credit m}^2 = \frac{200}{1,140} \times 262.59 = 46.07 \text{ m}^2$$

The sum of the Earned m² gives the total project progress in terms of square meters, which can then be converted to a percentage and is 59.96% for this example.

TABLE 6.1

Equivalent Units

Subtask	Allowed Credit	Total Units	Unit of Measure	Credit Quantity	Credit m²	Units to Date	Earned m²
Earthworks	0.03	3,000	m³	90.00	172.76	3,000	172.76
Foundations	0.06	1,540	m³	92.40	177.36	1,500	172.76
Roofing	0.12	1,140	m²	136.80	262.59	200	46.07
Floors	0.08	1,050	m²	84.00	161.24	450	69.10
Steelwork	0.20	300	Tons	60.00	115.17	300	115.17
Water connections	0.04	1	Each	0.04	0.08	1	0.08
Water piping	0.08	260	m	20.80	39.93	100	15.36
Ablutions	0.06	8	Each	0.48	0.92	0	0.00
Wiring	0.08	100	%	8.00	15.36	0	0.00
Air conditioners	0.10	4	Each	0.40	0.77	2	0.38
Lights and plugs	0.03	520	Each	15.60	29.94	100	5.76
Cleaning	0.01	144	Hours	1.44	2.76	0	0.00
Painting	0.11	100	%	11.00	21.11	10	2.11
Total	**1.00**	**8,167**		**520.96**	**1,000**	**5,663**	**599.55**

EV PITFALLS

Contracting and Earned Value

The EVM rules of credit are often impacted by the way in which the project work is contracted. On a fixed price type contract, the client has little interest in getting involved in the details of EVM measurements done by the contractor. The contractor has the responsibility for certain deliverables within the time and cost agreed in the contract. With this type of contract, any overruns will be for the contractor's account. To avoid surprises, the client may stipulate in the contract that the contractor should use EVM for project progress reporting and report on agreed incremental milestones.

On time-and-materials type contracts, the client is exposed to time and cost risks if the contractor does not perform and, therefore, wants visibility of the EVM of each control account. Table 6.2 gives a guideline of the rules of credit for different contract types.

TABLE 6.2

Progress Measurement Methods and Contract Types

Contract Type	Buyer	Seller
Fixed price contract types	• Incremental milestones • Start/finish • Cost ratio	• Units completed • Supervisor/resource estimate • Weighted or equivalent units
Time-and-materials, cost reimbursable, and remeasurable contract types	• Units completed • Supervisor/resource estimate • Weighted or equivalent units	• Units completed • Supervisor/resource estimate • Weighted or equivalent units

Cost Distribution

The project schedule is required to develop an integrated time and cost view of the project. To use EVM on a project the schedule must be baselined and resource-loaded to determine when resources will be required and when the cost for the resources will be incurred. This means that the estimated resources of the project must be associated with activities or deliverables to reflect when the project will consume the resource. All the commercially available project scheduling software packages allow one to assign resources to activities and to get a view of the spread of cost over the life of the project. The simplest approach is to apportion equal costs to each time period, in the same way that it was done in the first example. This may, however, not be the way in which it happens in reality. When material or equipment is purchased, the cost may be incurred as a once-off cost at the start of the task, while labor cost is usually distributed evenly over the duration of the task. In other instances, the material or equipment cost is only incurred at the end of the task. The way in which work is spread over the task duration may assume a nonlinear curve. The following examples illustrate the spread of cost over a task with a duration of 10 days:

Example: A task uses the following resources over a 10-day period:

• Labor: $1,500
• Material: $1,000
• Equipment: $500

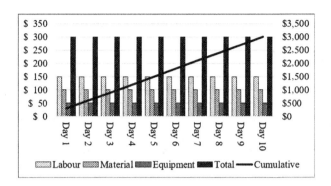

FIGURE 6.3
Scenario 1.

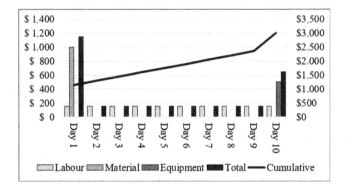

FIGURE 6.4
Scenario 2.

The following three scenarios (Figures 6.3–6.5 and Tables 6.3–6.5) show different ways of cost distribution. The manner in which the cost is distributed should be determined by the project team when the project is planned. The nature of the work and the purchase agreements (or contracts) will dictate the profile for allocation of each resource to the project.

In this example, the way in which the cost is apportioned to a task has a significant effect on the distribution of the cash flow. It will also have an impact on the way in which value is earned on the particular task and on the entire project. Table 6.6. shows the comparison of the PV for each of the above scenarios on days 2, 5, and 8.

The main driver for the allocation decision is when the value will be earned. This allocation usually depends on the perspective of the project scheduler. A second consideration is the way in which progress will be measured since progress measurement determines the EV.

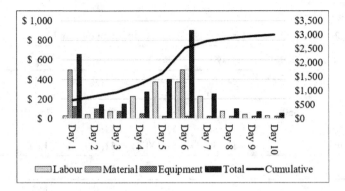

FIGURE 6.5
Scenario 3.

TABLE 6.3

Scenario 1: Linear Allocation

	Total	Day 1	Day 2	Day 3	Day 4	Day 5
Labor	$1,500	$150	$150	$150	$150	$150
Material	$1,000	$100	$100	$100	$100	$100
Equipment	$500	$50	$50	$50	$50	$50
Total	$3,000	$300	$300	$300	$300	$300
Cumulative		$300	$600	$900	$1,200	$1,500

	Day 6	Day 7	Day 8	Day 9	Day 10
Labor	$150	$150	$150	$150	$150
Material	$100	$100	$100	$100	$100
Equipment	$50	$50	$50	$50	$50
Total	$300	$300	$300	$300	$300
Cumulative	$1,800	$2,100	$2,400	$2,700	$3,000

In Scenario 2 above, the material is paid for on day 1, the labor is spread over the duration of the task, and the equipment is paid for on the last day. This is often the way in which a contractor who is performing work for a client looks at PV. The material is delivered on the first day and the contractor pays for it. The labor is paid for on a daily basis and the equipment may be rented and, therefore, paid at the end of the rental period. The contractor's client may not be interested in the day-to-day progress and only sees the value earned once the task is 100% complete. For this reason, it is suitable and often required for the client to have their own schedule for the project, which is a summary of the contractor's schedule. The rules of credit used by the client will also be different from those used by the contractor.

TABLE 6.4

Scenario 2: Linear Labor, Material on Day 1, and Equipment on Day 10

	Total	Day 1	Day 2	Day 3	Day 4	Day 5
Labor	$1,500	$150	$150	$150	$150	$150
Material	$1,000	$1,000	$0	$0	$0	$0
Equipment	$500	$0	$0	$0	$0	$0
Total	$3,000	$1,150	$150	$150	$150	$150
Cumulative		$1,150	$1,300	$1,450	$1,600	$1,750

	Day 6	Day 7	Day 8	Day 9	Day 10
Labor	$150	$150	$150	$150	$150
Material	$0	$0	$0	$0	$0
Equipment	$0	$0	$0	$0	$500
Total	$150	$150	$150	$150	$650
Cumulative	$1,900	$2,050	$2,200	$2,350	$3,000

TABLE 6.5

Scenario 3: Labor Ramps Up and then Ramps Down, Material 50% on Day 1, and 50%, Equipment Use Early

	Total	Day 1	Day 2	Day 3	Day 4	Day 5
Labor	$1,500	$30	$45	$75	$225	$375
Material	$1,000	$500	$0	$0	$0	$0
Equipment	$500	$125	$100	$75	$50	$25
Total	$3,000	$655	$145	$150	$275	$400
Cumulative		$655	$800	$950	$1,225	$1,625

	Day 6	Day 7	Day 8	Day 9	Day 10
Labor	$375	$225	$75	$45	$30
Material	$500	$0	$0	$0	$0
Equipment	$25	$25	$25	$25	$25
Total	$900	$250	$100	$70	$55
Cumulative	$2,525	$2,775	$2,875	$2,945	$3,000

TABLE 6.6

Comparison of PV in Scenarios 1–3

Scenario	Day 2	Day 5	Day 8
1	$600	$1,500	$2,400
2	$1,300	$1,750	$2,200
3	$800	$1,625	$2,875

When measuring the progress, each of the three resources (labor, material, and equipment) should be measured separately. The EV for the task is, therefore, the sum of the EV for the resources.

Reserves

The objective of using EVM is to ensure that the project is on time and within budget. One should, therefore, apply EVM to activities that should be monitored and that could, if not managed, cause the project to fall behind schedule or overshoot the budget. Within budget does not always imply the total project budget; it refers to the budgeted cost of the activities that are being monitored.

Applying EVM to activities that are in support of the main project work adds no value as far as the control of the project is concerned. Management activities seldom require EVM unless each management activity is budgeted and there is a real possibility that the estimated time and cost for these activities may overrun and impact on the project.

Contingency and Management Reserve funds should be excluded from the EVM system. These reserves cater for cost overruns and should only be brought into the EVM calculation if the funds have been allocated to a particular activity through the change control process. A change to the allocated budget for an activity requires the activity to be re-baselined, which changes the BAC for the activity as well as the project. If the contingency or management reserve is included in the PMB, any activity that is spending money according to its original estimate will appear to be underspending (CPI > 1) since the reserves are not used.

Critical Path EVM

The critical path of the project should receive special attention in EVM. Consider the following example. The Gantt chart in Figure 6.6 shows a small project. The critical path is shown in the "Critical" column, and the horizontal black lines indicate the progress made at the status date. The status date is indicated by the black arrow on the calendar days.

A few tasks are ahead of schedule as reflected in the calculations of Table 6.7. The total SPI is 1.24, which shows that the project is well ahead of schedule.

The project is, however, at risk of being late. This is not obvious from the summary EVM indicators but an analysis of the critical path makes it clear (Table 6.8).

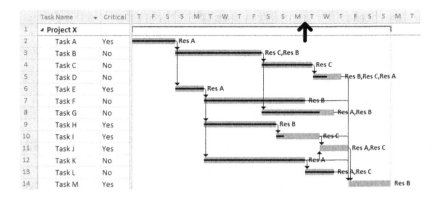

FIGURE 6.6

Critical path EVM.

TABLE 6.7

Project Earned Value Summary

Task Name	% Complete	BAC	PV	EV	SPI
Total	81%	$28,200	$18,540	$23,034	1.24
Task A	100%	$900	$900	$900	1.00
Task B	100%	$4,500	$4,500	$4,500	1.00
Task C	100%	$1,200	$960	$1,200	1.25
Task D	50%	$2,460	$0	$1,230	1.00
Task E	100%	$600	$600	$600	1.00
Task F	100%	$3,600	$3,600	$3,600	1.00
Task G	80%	$6,000	$3,600	$4,800	1.33
Task H	100%	$1,800	$1,800	$1,800	1.00
Task I	20%	$720	$480	$144	0.30
Task J	0%	$1,080	$0	$0	1.00
Task K	100%	$2,100	$2,100	$2,100	1.00
Task L	100%	$2,160	$0	$2,160	1.00
Task M	0%	$1,080	$0	$0	1.00

TABLE 6.8

Critical Path Summary

Task Name	% Complete	BAC	PV	BCWP	SPI
Total	81%	$6,180	$3,780	$3,444	0.91
Task A	100%	$900	$900	$900	1.00
Task E	100%	$600	$600	$600	1.00
Task H	100%	$1,800	$1,800	$1,800	1.00
Task I	20%	$720	$480	$144	0.30
Task J	0%	$1,080	$0	$0	1.00
Task M	0%	$1,080	$0	$0	1.00

It is easy to show that a project with an SPI greater than 1.0 will slip on the project delivery date. This is due to the fact that the activities on the critical path are behind schedule, but the value of these activities is relatively small compared to the rest of the project. The activities that are ahead of schedule and not on the critical path hide the fact that the project will finish late.

It is, therefore, a good practice to perform a separate EVM analysis on the critical path of the project. Two useful calculations can be performed with this information. The first is the percentage of value on the critical path. In the above example, this value is:

$$CP_{value} = \frac{BAC_{cp}}{BAC} \times 100 = \frac{\$6,180}{\$28,200} \times 100 = 21.9\% \qquad (6.23)$$

where CP_{value} is the percentage of the total project value that is on the critical path, BAC_{cp} is the total estimated cost of the activities on the critical path, and BAC is the total project estimated cost. The second calculation is the total number of activities on the critical path:

$$CP_{activities} = \frac{critical\,path\,activities}{project\,activities} \times 100 = \frac{6}{13} \times 100 = 46.2\% \qquad (6.24)$$

The example given above has a very large percentage of critical path activities and, therefore, has a high risk of a critical path activity being delayed. A project with low values for the percentage value of the critical path and the percentage activities on the critical path is clearly less risky.

CONCLUSION

In this chapter, the principles of EVM were discussed and several pitfalls were highlighted. Earned value can be used on almost any project and is a useful tool to give exact numerical data about the performance of a project. The biggest mistake made by project teams when using EVM is not setting up the project correctly, and this is the main reason why project practitioners in some industries believe that EVM is not suitable for their project or industry.

REFERENCES

Fleming, Q. W., and Koppelman, J. M. (2010). *Earned Value Project Management* (4th edn). Newtown Square, PA: Project Management Institute, Inc.

Lipke, W. H. (2009). *Earned Schedule*. United States: Lulu Publishing.

TechAmerica. (2013). *Earned Value Management Systems*. Washington, DC: TechAmerica.

7

How to Manage Big Data Issues in a Project Environment

Ryan Legard

CONTENTS

PREPARING FOR A DATA DELUGE

As organizations and project teams make the decision to begin collecting and analyzing large amounts of data, the initial flood of information can seem overwhelming. They may wish to collect customer and user data, cost data, schedule data, program performance metrics, and technical performance measurements; regardless of data type, the experience will always be the same—the prepared will succeed while the unprepared will find themselves lost in the sea of data, eventually reverting back to ignoring its existence, or drawing hasty conclusions with incomplete or inaccurate data. There exist deliberate steps that organizations and project teams must undertake to ensure they are prepared to collect and ingest data, interpret its meaning, and draw actionable conclusions to achieve business goals. Managing big data and generating actionable insights in a project environment becomes a challenge of aligning project-specific goals with organizational and business goals. To do so, the organization and project teams must first take steps to ensure appropriate levels of maturity and readiness are in place.

A central tenet of organizational readiness involves establishing mechanisms for data collection. Basic program management and data management discipline must exist before the data collected will be of high enough quality to allow for actionable insight. The siren's song of big data has lured countless companies into feeling a false sense of empowerment. Collecting data alone does not lead to better decision-making, though it is an important first step in the right direction. Data has a story to tell, but it is the job of analysts, data scientists, and the project team to act as the interpreter. In the nascent stages of readiness, it is easy to miss the message. Indeed, drawing conclusions with poor data can provide a false sense of security, leading decision-makers to choose a path worse than following gut instinct alone.

Within the academic community there exists a contentious debate surrounding the first usage or the origin of the words "big data." Some researchers trace its first usage back to the early twenty-first century, as Douglas Laney wrote of big data in a publication. Others trace the origins of big data to earlier, in the mid-1990s where John Mashey, a scientist with Silicon Graphics, reportedly discussed the topic repeatedly (Lohr, 2013). Regardless of its precise origins, big data is now a widely used buzzword in business settings. However common the phrase, the classification and delineation of big data, as compared to traditional data, is more nebulous.

In general terms, big data displays several key characteristics, commonly referred to as the "Three V's." The existence of three specific attributes differentiates big data from other types of data. These attributes include volume, variety, and velocity (Laney, 2001).

1. *Volume*—Big data includes extremely large amounts of data measured in terabytes to numbers measured in petabytes (1,024 terabytes). The sheer size rules out conventional data analysis methods in many cases.
2. *Variety*—High degrees of variation exist between data types. Big data not just comprises numbers, but it includes text, audio, images, and video in structured, semi-structured, and unstructured formats.

3. *Velocity*—Data is generated and must be analyzed at a tremendously fast rate. New data points are generated every fraction of a second, requiring the capability to store and analyze ever-increasing amounts of information.

In the twenty-first century, we are generating data at a pace unparalleled in human history. In a world where every mouse click or key stroke generates a data point, the mechanisms to analyze gigantic data sets have changed to accommodate such an enormous scale. Beginning the journey with the decision to use big data to inform project management and business decisions is an important first step, but the actions that follow must be deliberate. A regimented approach is necessary to ensure data collection and analysis goals align with business goals and objectives. Getting an initial sense of how the project team should and will use data provides the foundation for successful data-driven project management. Begin this journey by asking and answering the following:

- When are we ready to begin collecting data?
- Why do we wish to capture this data?
- How will we use and analyze the results?
- What is our desired outcome or business goal?

BIG DATA CHALLENGES AT THE PROJECT LEVEL

Project teams function as smaller entities within a larger organization. As such, a disconnect often exists between the insight the project team hopes to gain from analyzing big data and the overarching goals and objectives of the business as a whole. Even though the project team may like their approach to managing big data and the direction of their analytical endeavors, they must consider the overarching business goals or objectives at the organizational level, or all their hard work may be for naught.

Project teams encounter numerous barriers as they seek to enlighten their organization with their tamed data and analytical insights. These challenges are typically attributable to four sources: people, processes, technology, and data. Gradual maturity in each of these areas will ultimately allow the project team to succeed. However, seemingly endless challenges fill the journey along the way. Common challenges or obstacles to big data analysis in a project environment include the following:

- Difficulty identifying an appropriate starting point
- Technological barriers (storage, computing, data analytics software)
- Challenges in pairing data with an appropriate analytical method
- Organizational immaturity
- Lack of stakeholder buy-in
- Management inability to understand the value of data analysis
- Lack of responsibility and clearly defined roles
- Data-specific challenge, including biases in data and data collection methods

By considering common challenges they are likely to encounter, the project team can position themselves for success and identify and overcome obstacles before they emerge as roadblocks. To fully understand each of these challenges and the strategies to overcome them, we will explore each of them in depth.

DETERMINING WHERE TO START

As with any aspirational endeavor, the first hurdle project teams may encounter as they begin to analyze data is often confusion surrounding where to even start. The axiom "well begun is half done" holds true when attempting to harness big data in a project environment. When organizations and project teams begin efforts to collect and analyze data, they may be pleasantly surprised. In most cases, an abundance of data already exists, often in readily available and ingestible form. However, to derive the most utility and insight from existing data, the project team must first identify a starting point, a strategy, and a desired outcome. The project team should begin by assessing the type or categorization of data that is available.

Data fits into three general types or categories: structured data, unstructured data, and semi-structured data. The data type has tremendous ramifications on the analysis method(s) available for application. Table 7.1 identifies these data type groupings and some common characteristics of each.

Structured and semi-structured data will require the lowest level of effort to derive actionable insight from. However, only an estimated 5%

TABLE 7.1

Data Types

Structured Data	Semi-Structured Data	Unstructured Data
Data type typically found in databases or data warehouses	Data typically found in CSV, XML, or JavaScript Object Notation (JSON) format or file extensions	Typically, data in the form of raw text or multimedia (images, video)
Data is stored in rows and columns, may be text or numerical in nature	Not structured neatly in rows and columns	Not structured neatly in rows and columns
A relational key can be mapped to fields (one to one or one to many)	Requires additional work to get the data into a relational database format	Requires extensive work to catalog and translate into structured data
Simple to retrieve information through querying	Queries must be very structured, for example, through Boolean method (AND, OR, NOT)	Often qualitative in nature rather than quantitative
Often a backup, or multiple backup copies, of the data exist	May require multiple formulae merged to arrive at desired output	A common example includes social media data

of the existing data falls into the structured category (Cukier, 2010). The more common unstructured data requires human decoding and categorization, or the introduction of sophisticated computing algorithms to identify patterns, catalog, and transformation of the data into a more usable semistructured or structured data type. These endeavors of migrating from unstructured to structured data can be time-consuming and costly. For these reasons, as a project team begins embarking on its journey into data analytics, it is easiest to begin with structured or "clean" data, a type neatly organized into rows and columns. This strategy minimizes upfront work and expenses and helps to ensure that the project team does not lose its momentum at the start.

In addition to carefully considering data format or data type, data availability is an important variable to weigh during this initial phase. Beginning by collecting and analyzing readily available data lowers the barrier to entry and helps to ensure the project team does not grow immediately weary of complicated analysis efforts. The project team should seek to separate unusable data, or data that does not align to a business objective, from the data sets they wish to analyze. This method of data cleansing helps to limit data storage needs, while also reducing the time to analyze large data sets. Readily available data may include data sets already owned by the project team or those owned by other groups within the same organization. Reliance on external organizations to provide data will increase the timeline for analysis, introduce data governance and management challenges, and complicate communication channels. Once the team selects the data sets they wish to analyze, the next step is to select an appropriate analytical method.

PAIRING DATA WITH AN ANALYTICAL METHOD

Early big data analysis efforts in a project environment lend themselves best to the use of an analytical method at the beginning of the readiness spectrum. This approach minimizes the upfront investment necessary to gain insight from data and provides a gradual runway for the data analysis team to evolve methods, incorporate lessons learned, and gain buy-in from project stakeholders. In some cases, the project team can leverage early successes to provide the justification for the organization to increase or continue capital expenditures on advanced technologies. Figure 7.1 displays a range of common analytical methods aligned along a maturity spectrum.

Not all analysis methods will be appropriate for a given data set, as big data is a relative term encompassing a tremendous variation in data set sizes. Cost typically increases as the complexity and maturity of the

Analytical Method

Statistical Analysis	Data Mining	Regression Modeling	Clustering	Machine Learning	Deep Learning	Quantum Computing
Analyzing data sets to identify patterns, trends, and uncover relationships between variables	Sifting through large amounts of raw data to identify trends and patterns; process may be automated or semiautomated	Establishing a mathematical model to represent the relationship between multiple variables, eventually seeking to enable predictive analytics	Data mining methodology that entails grouping of extremely large data sets, usually through advanced computing algorithms	Using artificial intelligence to generate and apply sophisticated and adaptive algorithms to data sets, with limited or no human interaction	Variation of machine learning that allows for pattern recognition in unstructured data sets	Capable of exponentially faster and more complex data analysis than traditional computers. Serves as the most powerful enabling technology for machine learning and artificial intelligence

Increasing Complexity and Maturity

Basic Analytical Methods	Advanced Analytical Methods	State of the Art

FIGURE 7.1
Analytical methods.

analytical methods increase. Deep learning and quantum computing require purchasing or leasing expensive infrastructure; however, if harnessed correctly, these approaches can yield some of the highest return on investment, as analysis is orders of magnitude more rapid than conventional methods. Indeed, as technology evolves, talented data scientists can derive meaningful insight from data much quicker than before.

BIG DATA TECHNOLOGIES

Basic levels of project management and organizational discipline must be in place to set up the project team and data analysts for success. Once project management discipline is in place, the project team will need some level of capital investment from the organization to enable data analysis efforts. Technologies for managing big data have progressed in leaps and bounds over the past decade. However, this also introduces new challenges. For example, as storage becomes cheaper with the emergence of new technologies, there exists the natural urge to capture any and all data because it comes at a low cost. Organizations and project teams must fight this urge, and only seek to capture data that aligns with a specific purpose—to meet a project or business goal. Table 7.2 identifies common technologies for storing data.

Organizations will pair big data storage technologies with analytics offerings that allow the organization to draw insight from the data that they store. Many service providers for big data storage technologies include analytics offerings, which ensure platform compatibility. Table 7.3 identifies common technologies for big data analytics.

The decision to select a particular platform or technology will vary by organization. Most organizations are looking for technical solutions that are scalable, secure, provide high availability and reliability, with low latency, but trade-offs are often necessary to separate requirements from "nice to haves," and arrive at solutions that can fit within a defined budget. Organizations should perform a full business case analysis to determine their storage, computing, and analytics needs. These decisions on technologies will then flow down to the individual project team. In most organizations, leadership may consult individual project team members, but otherwise there may exist limited opportunities to influence decisions to purchase technologies for big data storage and analysis. Ultimately, the project team can influence

TABLE 7.2

Big Data Storage Technologies

Technology	Description	Advantages	Disadvantages
Data warehouse or enterprise data warehouse (EDW)	• Serves as a central repository for data • Stores data in files and folders for "cleaner" data sets	• Allows for reporting, analysis, and mining • Can store historical and current data • Can establish business rules to only store data that serve a business purpose	• Challenges in loading data from disparate data sources • Entails a long-term commitment to see any cost efficiencies
Data lake	• Provides capability to store data in its existing format • Stores structured, unstructured semi-structured data all at the same time	• Can pair with data mining and analytics tools for querying • Queries can drill down into relevant data • Data analysts can structure unique queries, not subject to same rigidity as data warehouses	• Requires organizational maturity to fight urge to dump all data into a data lake • Must pay attention to archival or removal of data or querying becomes increasingly complex
Cloud storage	• Remote servers are used to store data that users access via the Internet	• Able to buy more storage space and quickly scale-up or -down based on demand • Simplified backup and recovery • Easy to add and remove users	• Some organizations may have security concerns associated with the cloud • Difficult to switch service providers • As uptime guarantees increase (e.g., 99.9%–99.99%) so does cost
Hybrid cloud storage	• Storage method that blends Cloud storage with on-site or local storage	• Offers a stepping stone for organizations not yet ready to fully commit to the Cloud • Can host frequently used data locally to reduce latency, then store backups or less frequently used data in the Cloud • Provides flexibility to scale to accommodate short-term spikes in demand	• Significantly higher cost than a pure Cloud model • Physical infrastructure will need to be upgraded or replaced frequently • Potential compatibility challenges between local storage and Cloud host technologies

TABLE 7.3

Big Data Analytics Technologies

Technology	Description	Advantages	Disadvantages
Analytics in the Cloud	• Cloud-based software as a service (SaaS) and business intelligence capabilities used to analyze large data sets hosted in the Cloud	• Cost effective, as pricing is typically pay-per-use • Very scalable solution allowing for the rapid addition and removal of accounts and users	• Commercially available or open source capabilities are less customizable than in-house analytics solutions • Attempts to build in-house Cloud analytics capabilities can be very time-consuming
Not Only SQL (NoSQL) analytics tools	• Typically, a Cloud-based analytics capability that allows for analysis of less structured data types	• Provides flexibility to analyze data that is not in a relational database format (e.g., JSON or XML files)	• Traditional SQL queries have difficulty returning meaningful data, complicating concurrent use of SQL-based visualization and analytics technologies

the technical direction of the organization by employing best practices at the project level, identifying weaknesses and opportunities with legacy systems, and providing these insights to leadership.

DRIVING ORGANIZATIONAL MATURITY AND PROCESS DISCIPLINE

Big data analysis efforts at the project level will face significant challenges without proper controls in place at the organizational level to act as success enablers. These controls, commonly referred to as processes, serve as a series of consistent and repeatable steps that the team applies continuously throughout the entire project lifecycle. At the earliest stages of organizational maturity, processes may exist on an ad hoc basis, as project teams may apply processes inconsistently from project to project. During the early stages of organizational maturity, the organization may not document processes in a formal fashion. As organizations progress to levels

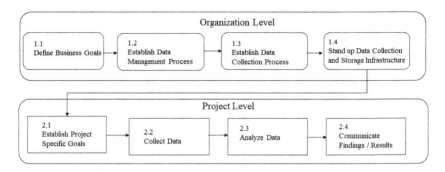

FIGURE 7.2
Process flow down.

of increasing maturity, they begin formally documenting processes, which then flow down to the individual project teams. Figure 7.2 illustrates the concept of process flow down from the organizational level to the project level.

Before the project team can be successful in their data analysis endeavors, there must exist overarching business goals and management processes at the organizational level. Additionally, the basic technical infrastructure for data analysis must be in place to provide the project team with the technology necessary to perform advanced analytics. Once these overarching goals, processes, and enabling steps are in place, the project team can undertake a disciplined, regimented approach to data analysis. Eventually, this comes full circle, as the project team shares insights back up to the management levels in the organization.

To enable gradually more sophisticated analysis, the project team must introduce and instill discipline into project management practices. The project team can help to drive organizational maturity, or overcome the hurdle, by employing the following approaches:

- Begin by identifying a type of data for analysis along with a desired outcome
- Focus on readily available data that is structured or semi-structured in nature
- Use discipline at the project team level to drive bottom-up organizational discipline

Transformative and meaningful change does not happen overnight. It also does not occur without setbacks. Project-level discipline is vital to ensure that the organization as a whole does not grow weary of big data collection and analysis efforts. Many project and organizational maturity models exist. Each model seeks to establish a disciplined and repeatable process to gradual maturity, across a variety of spectrums. Typically, organizational maturity models focus on four criteria: people, process, technology, and data. A critical point of emphasis and an overarching commonality between maturity models is the recognition of the gradual and iterative nature of change.

Process discipline can come from the top-down, beginning at senior leadership levels, eventually making its way down to individual project managers and project teams, or it can be a bottom-up movement. Organizational change is difficult; accordingly, some of the most effective changes can occur at the project level, where the project team can test processes and approaches on a smaller, more controlled scale. Project managers and project teams can begin introducing process discipline at their levels by performing a preliminary gap analysis or gap assessment. This entails looking at areas where processes are undocumented, nonexistent, or lacking, and identifying methods to close these gaps. With the gap analysis method, the project team or organization will identify an implementation status—fully implemented, partially implemented, and not implemented—against each process or subprocess area. The organization or project team can perform gap analyses across all process areas to establish an understanding of the "as-is" state, or process baseline, and the steps necessary to close gaps to reach the ideal "to-be" state. The organization or project team should repeat this analysis on a regular basis, such as annually, to monitor how process discipline progresses. Gaps that exist at the organizational level are often different from the gaps that exist at the project level; accordingly, it is often beneficial to analyze process gaps at both levels, driving toward greater maturity in tandem.

GAINING STAKEHOLDER BUY-IN

Some of the biggest hurdles to harnessing big data will come from within the organization itself. Project stakeholders, both internal and external, must understand the objective of project data analysis at the beginning; otherwise they may emerge as detractors. The project team may lean heavily on stakeholders as enablers for their analysis efforts to succeed.

For instance, if the project team seeks to gain more insight into the project's cost performance, they will rely on the organization's finance and accounting teams to provide historical data, up-to-date actuals, and subject matter expertise along the way.

If the project team cannot concisely articulate the intent and perceived benefits of their analysis, they are more likely to encounter resistance. The project team can gain buy-in from stakeholders by following the approaches listed below:

- Identify all stakeholders (internal and external) as early as possible
- List the roles of each stakeholder and their criticality to project success
- Communicate intentions to each stakeholder
- Anticipate areas of concern or pushback
- Identify what each stakeholder may wish to gain in return for their support
- List benefits tailored to each specific stakeholder
- Anticipate any risks associated with the approach

Nobody likes to feel blindsided or surprised. By involving project stakeholders early and often and communicating intentions and benefits, the project team can gain buy-in and leverage stakeholders as advocates for their data analysis efforts. Inherently, all project stakeholders have some capacity to affect the outcome of a project. When approached properly, the project team can turn stakeholders into champions for their efforts, rather than detractors. Success or failure ultimately depends largely on the project team's ability to effectively communicate the benefits, or the value statement, to each stakeholder.

COMMUNICATING THE VALUE STATEMENT

Once the project team has approached all project stakeholders with their vision of data-informed management, they must next envision how to communicate their findings to the leadership in the organization, keeping them apprised of progress along the way. If the project team wishes to gain management buy-in, particularly at the senior leadership levels, they must identify methods to communicate large amounts of data in a concise manner. The project team must tailor graphics, visualizations, and dashboards to the needs and preferences of the audience. Most C-suite and staff at senior leadership levels have busy schedules and a shortage of free time. While the extensive data analysis the project team has performed may impress senior leadership, the C-suite will not have the abundant free time necessary to dive deeply into every specific detail. Accordingly, when presenting to this audience, the project team must look for data visualization methods that are informative but also easy to quickly digest and interpret.

One of the most frequently used communication methods for leadership audiences is Microsoft PowerPoint or a similar software that allows for the creation of presentation slides. PowerPoint slide presentations should contain a mix of text and data visualizations. To help senior leadership understand the value of big data analysis, the project team should summarize the value statement in a "bottom line up front" fashion early in the presentation. Any text on slides should provide necessary background, but the team can effectively communicate data through data visualizations. Preferred data visualization methods vary by industry and organization; however, some general rules can help to ensure the audience is receptive to the presentation.

- *Include a legend and label all axes*: Legends and axis labels should be descriptive. If a metric is percentage based, be sure to include additional information, such as percentage of a whole, percent growth year-over-year, and so on.
- *Avoid obscure visualizations*: A circular area chart may look great to a data scientist, but instantly serve as a turnoff for senior leadership.
- *Stick to two axes*: 3 D visualizations utilizing x, y, and z axes are difficult to interpret when flattened onto a two-dimensional piece of paper.
- *Be mindful of colors that a color-blind audience member cannot see*: Try not to use red and green together. If absolutely necessary, use drastically different shades, such as a very light red and a very dark green.
- *Add gridlines where appropriate to allow for easy comparison*: Axes should start at zero and progress in regular intervals. Tick marks on axes or gridlines in the chart area can help to draw the eye to points of reference more quickly.
- *When using bar charts, space bars appropriately*: Spaces between bars should be equal to half the width of the bars themselves.

ASSIGNING RESPONSIBILITY

The rise of big data has generated a new job title across many organizations—the chief data officer (CDO) or chief analytics officer (CAO). Regardless of the job title, the intent remains the same; this is an individual who has the concentrated authority across the enterprise and control over all items that relate to data. The CDO or CAO exists to provide a data governance structure, centralized authority, and ensure proper change management processes and collection procedures are in place for data. The chief data officer also bears responsibility for ensuring the appropriate levels of privacy, security, and protection of data. This individual is often the mechanism for providing the necessary technical infrastructure to enable analytics more broadly across the organization. At the project level, there is a constant challenge to adequately and appropriately define roles of all team members. The existence of a CDO helps to ensure the organization implements a consistent approach to data analysis, but this role may also complicate the delineation between what the project team is responsible for and what the CDO must manage.

Since big data often crosses functional areas, this creates a new source of confusion within the project team. Ideally, the project team should identify a singular point of contact who bears responsibility for each major process area and action. To ensure their analytical pursuits are successful, the project team needs to identify who is responsible, accountable, consulted, and informed for major processes and decisions. A RACI matrix is a valuable tool in creating clear boundaries for the project team and helping to avoid duplication of effort. The acronym RACI stands for responsible, accountable, consulted, and informed. To ensure there is no confusion over assignment categorization, it is helpful to understand the definition of each role.

- *Responsible*: The responsible person is in charge of executing the described task. Every task should have a person identified as responsible.
- *Accountable*: The accountable person may have signoff authority or otherwise have final approval authority for the specific task or assignment. Every assignment should have a person marked as accountable.
- *Consulted*: The consulted person may be a subject matter expert who weighs in or provides input on a task. Often, an assignment cannot move forward until all consulted parties provide input.

- *Informed*: The informed person is looped in on final decisions; however, unlike those consulted, the informed individual does not weigh in on the task or activity.

Table 7.4 provides an overview of a notional RACI matrix. The key with any RACI matrix is to ensure that there is not diffusion of responsibility. Whenever possible, responsibility for any given assignment should reside with one individual. Additionally, key roles like that of the project manager should always have some involvement in the decision-making process, even if it just involves receiving information at the end of the task, in the informed role.

Assigning multiple responsible or accountable parties for the same activity can create confusion. The overarching goal of the RACI matrix, also commonly described as a responsibility assignment matrix (RAM), is to provide the mechanism to ensure the roles of each team member are communicated clearly, appropriately delineated, and no confusion exists due to overlapping functions. Every box in a RACI matrix does not need to contain an assignment. In some cases, an individual may not have any role in a task or activity. By employing best practices like centralizing authority and responsibility, and using mechanisms like the RACI matrix or responsibility assignment matrix, the project team helps to ensure that there exists a clear understanding of who does what and who bears the responsibility for ensuring successful completion of a task or assignment.

TABLE 7.4

RACI Matrix

| | Employee Role or Title | | | | |
Activity Description	Chief Data Officer	Project Manager	Data Scientist	Data Management Specialist	Lead Engineer
Provide technical infrastructure	R	I	C	C	A
Develop data analytics techniques	A	I	R	C	C
Identify project goals and objectives	I	R	A	I	A
Establish project data storage environment	C	I	A	R	A

OVERCOMING DATA-RELATED CHALLENGES

As analysts seek to derive meaning from mountains of data, a natural tendency exists to develop observations and identify the existence of patterns very early in the collection process. Hypothesis generation entails identifying the existence of patterns based upon a limited subset or sample of data. Indeed, this approach is a cornerstone of the scientific method, and not inherently problematic. However, this method of thinking gives rise to opportunities that introduce multiple forms of bias into data collection methods.

Bias in data collection is most common during the early stages of organizational and data analysis maturity, as humans are heavily involved throughout all processes. However, even minimizing the role of humans in big data analysis does not fully *eliminate* the risk of bias emerging. Once computers and machine learning algorithms handle the lion's share of analysis efforts, biases become less prevalent, provided the inputs include varied data sources. However, opportunities for the emergence of bias inevitably exist during all stages of data analysis. Biases in data and data collection methods can include the following:

- *Availability bias*: Tendency to latch on to the first pattern that emerges in data analysis or to ascribe undue value to hypotheses that are easy to recall from recent memory (e.g., a previous analysis of a data set);
- *Confirmation bias*: Occurs when an analyst seeks out data to confirm his or her hypothesis, while dismissing data that does not support the hypothesis. This bias may be active (known to the analyst) or passive (a subconscious tendency);
- *Selection bias*: Selection of data sets or sources that are not truly randomized or representative of the overall population.

While no singular method will eliminate bias from big data analysis, acknowledging the existence or possibility of bias is extremely important. Data analysts, scientists, and project team members should seek out data from varied sources to broaden sample size and introduce multiple collection methods. Introducing control variables into the analysis can help to eliminate confounding or lurking variables from distorting hypotheses. The project team can leverage process discipline, such as the creation and adherence to data management and data collection processes, to limit the impact bias may have on analytical efforts.

SUMMARY

The project environment is fraught with challenges that seek to emerge as roadblocks as the team harnesses the power of big data. Across each area—people, processes, technology, and data—there are strategies that the team can employ to minimize the likelihood of issues getting in the way of their goals. Table 7.5 summarizes approaches described in this chapter to help guide the project team along, as they step over obstacle after obstacle.

TABLE 7.5

Big Data Issues and Resolutions

Challenge/Issue	Resolution
1. Difficulty identifying an appropriate starting point	• Seek to begin analyzing readily available, structured or semi-structured data • Use early successes to build management buy-in and justify further expenditures for big data analysis
2. Technological barriers	• Resist urge to store and capture all data, only collect data that serves a business purpose • Perform an analysis of alternatives, evaluating pros and cons of each storage, compute, and analytics platform • Focus on scalability to ensure the technology will continue to serve its purpose as data sets and the number of users and analysts grows
3. Challenges pairing data with an analytical method	• Select an analytical method that matches the data type and the maturity of the project and organization
4. Organizational immaturity	• Perform a gap analysis to isolate and identify areas for improvement, then repeat the analysis at regular intervals • Drive organizational maturity from the bottom-up by following industry best practices in project management
5. Lack of stakeholder buy-in	• Communicate intentions, benefits, and risks early and often • Anticipate areas of stakeholder pushback and prepare rebuttals that emphasize benefits and opportunities
6. Management is unable to understand the value of big data analysis	• Map project-specific goals pertaining to big data to overarching organizational goals • Summarize messages in a "bottom line upfront" manner • Use data visualization tools to provide concise visualizations

(Continued)

TABLE 7.5 (*Continued*)

Big Data Issues and Resolutions

Challenge/Issue	Resolution
7. Lack or responsibility and clearly defined roles	• Recommend creation of a chief data officer position for centralized authority • Create a RACI or RAM matrix to clearly delineate roles and responsibilities within the project team and broader organization
8. Data-specific challenges	• Understand that some degree of bias will always be present • Minimize bias by analyzing data from multiple and randomized sources, gathered through a variety of collection methods • Eliminate confounding variables through the introduction of control variables

REFERENCES

Cukier, Kenneth. "Data, Data Everywhere." *The Economist*, February 27, 2010. Accessed October 3, 2017. www.economist.com/node/15557443.

Laney, Doug. 3-D Data Management: Controlling Data Volume, Velocity and Variety Application Delivery Strategies. META Group Inc., February 6, 2001, p. 949. Accessed August 1, 2018. www.blogs.gartner.com/doug-laney/files/2012/01/ad949-3D-Data-Management-Controlling-Data-Volume-Velocity-and-Variety.pdf.

Lohr, Steve. "The Origins of 'Big Data': An Etymological Detective Story." *The New York Times*, February 1, 2013. Accessed August 7, 2017. www.bits.blogs.nytimes.com/2013/02/01/the-origins-of-big-data-an-etymological-detective-story/.

8

IT Solutions of Data Analytics as Applied to Project Management

Michael Bragen

CONTENTS

INTRODUCTION

It's a prevailing truth that software projects are risky ventures. Across industries, technologies, and geographies, projects have a failure rate of around 30%. Considering that the global cost of write-offs, lost opportunity costs, and out-of-pocket waste is measured in hundreds of billions of dollars annually, the impact is significant on the world economy.

According to the Standish Group, a research advisory firm that publishes reports detailing software mishaps, there are variations in failure rate. Large projects are more prone to failure. Some methodologies yield better results. Complexity, and other factors related to the type, environment, and staff experience affect outcomes. But the bottom line remains bleak: despite a plethora of strategies, management techniques, and education, the drumbeat of failure and cancellations has continued at about the same rate for decades.

The solution to this universal problem lies in the practice of IT governance. Governance refers to the set of policies, functions, processes, procedures, and responsibilities that define the establishment, management, and control of projects and portfolios. Process visibility, enabled by data, is a key to governance. Analytics, therefore, provides a foundation for control and improvement.

In this chapter, we will address the following key questions about applying data analytics to project management:

- Why does analytics matter in project management?
- What is the role of governance and can data support it?
- What's at stake for organizations, in terms of project risk and exposure?
- What makes for an effective governance tool?
- What data should we measure, and why?
- How do organizations get started with data analytics?
- What are the challenges for implementation of a risk mitigation and governance solution?
- What are the essential capabilities for a data analytics solution?
- What is the future of data analytics for project management?

SETTING THE STAGE

What's a Project? And What Do We Mean by Success?

The Project Management Institute defines a project as "a temporary endeavor undertaken to create a unique product or service." Qualifying examples abound in industry, but most share the concept that a project is a series of tasks that need to be completed in order to reach a specific outcome, or as a set of inputs and outputs required to achieve a particular goal. This chapter focuses on attributes of and influences on information technology (IT) projects. It's worthy of note that applying these influences to non-IT projects may serve to mitigate risk as well. While it would be interesting to examine how data analytics applies to, say, road construction projects, it's beyond scope of this chapter to do so.

In the world of information technology, a project is successful if it meets the needs of the "customer" or principal stakeholder. IT project goals include automation of business tasks and functions within subobjectives of scope, duration, budget, and quality. The objective of every project organization must include S.M.A.R.T. (specific, measurable, achievable, realistic, and timely) goals. Aside from the actual construction of automated functionality, meeting these objectives is nontechnical in nature. Success, ultimately, depends on the application of management principles to achieve goals.

Early Warning Signs of Project Failure

Success is elusive. On average, only about a third of IT projects meet user needs and are completed on time and on budget (Figure 8.1). The situation is worse with large and/or complex projects than with small efforts.

Ongoing research into the reasons behind the poor track record for projects yields a consistent set of influences. Recent studies by Professor Leon A. Kappelman and others report lists of significant factors that management can use to determine (before it's too late) that a project is in danger of failure. Early warning signs of project failure. Table 8.1 shows Kappelman's list of the "deadly dozen," organized by the party primarily responsible for control or contribution.

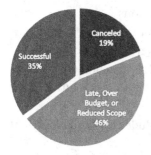

FIGURE 8.1
Two-thirds of projects fail.

TABLE 8.1

Significant Factors for Failure

Management (Executive)	Management (Team)	Team	Customer
Lack of top management support	Weak project manager	Weak commitment by the project team	Insufficient stakeholder involvement
Resources assigned to a higher priority project	Ineffective schedule planning and/or management	Team members lack requisite knowledge and/or skills	Subject matter experts overscheduled
No business case for the project	No change control process or change management		Lack of documented requirements and/or success criteria
	Communication breakdown among stakeholders		

In particular, communication deficiency (in other words, lack of a formal medium for information transfer) between stakeholders is a common risk factor that has a cascading effect on projects.

Understanding the most significant factors that cause failure provides a foundation for predictive analytics. By evaluating the team, environment, and projects in an organization in terms of these factors, it is possible to anticipate problems while they can still be corrected. Early warning signs (EWS) analysis is an important component in IT governance.

Data-Driven Governance

"Good governance practice" means clear and continual communication to enable understanding of project status and issue resolution. The most important parameters of governance include the following:

- Well-defined reviews and approvals for decisions
- An archive of decisions and issue resolution for management review (for alignment with business strategy, and key business objectives)
- Clear roles, responsibilities, and objectives for stakeholders
- A structured process for decision-making and issue resolution

Any attempt to mitigate risks and issues must include clear and consistent communication channels for all involved:

FIGURE 8.2
Control room architecture.

- Customers and users (or their surrogates, typically business analysts)
- Development team members (programmers, analysts, quality assurance, and testers)
- Product or delivery managers
- Senior management (customer and developer organization)

Conceptually, the need for communication across these entities can be addressed by deployment of centralized "control rooms" to monitor issues and broadcast status to stakeholders in (near) real time.

The conceptual "always-on control room" (Figure 8.2) comprises an expert knowledge system rule base combined with operational (project) information. Like an airplane cockpit, the control room provides a visual representation of key points of status (and failure). It is the system of record for status, decision-making, and governance support information. Control rooms feed repositories of data (for maintenance of historical information that is used to adjust algorithms and processes). A configurable dashboard system typically provides analytics and views of the data to stakeholders on demand.

ANALYTICS TOOL SOLUTIONS

Project Management

The basic process of managing projects, defined by the *Project Management Body of Knowledge* (PMBOK) published by the Project Management Institute, establishes the measurement of project progress as a critical success factor. Project progress must be measured regularly to identify variances from the plan as well as to determine when the project is finished.

Variances are fed into the control processes in the various knowledge areas. To the extent that significant variances are observed (i.e., those that jeopardize the project objectives), adjustments to the plan are made by repeating the appropriate project planning processes. PMBOK refers to a number of key processes for controlling projects:

- *Progress measurement and reporting*: Collecting and disseminating progress information
- *Scope change management*: Documenting and controlling changes to project scope
- *Quality control*: Measuring project deliverables and activities to assess whether quality objectives are being met
- *Quality improvement*: Evaluating project performance on a regular basis to determine how to improve project quality
- *Time/schedule control*: Controlling and responding to schedule changes
- *Cost control*: Controlling and responding to cost changes
- *Risk control*: Responding to changes in risk over the course of the project

Looking Backward vs. Looking Forward

Typical project management software applications are used to log effort (hours worked) against a series of tasks and across resources. These tools are useful for reporting status, tracking effort, balancing resources, and managing dependencies among tasks and staff. Management relies on this information to account for progress made against objectives and budgets. It's important to recognize that this project tracking information is focused on the recent past as well as history.

On the other hand, tools that use data supporting early warning signs (EWS) analysis are used to avoid disastrous projects. These tools are designed to identify causes of project failure within the first part (20% of the original project schedule). In other words, the goal is to provide warning of failure risk while there is still time to get back on a track toward success, at a reasonable cost. Management control rooms equipped with EWS data provide information to stakeholders about the following aspects:

- Impending and imminent points of failure on projects (or across projects)
- Proximity to the "point of no return" for projects that should be canceled due to unrecoverable loss of value

- Suggested actions to mitigate risks of errors
- Audit trails and trendlines

As such, data about projects can be separated into backward-looking "lagging indicators" (most useful for tracking progress) and forward-looking "leading indicators" (most useful for managing risk). Managing risk cannot be done effectively by relying solely on lagging indicators. A tool that provides views of what has already happened is like the rearview mirror in a car. Using this information to steer a project will cause problems.

What Metrics Should Be Monitored?

The purpose of governance and project management control is to manage the conditions that cause defects to occur, and allow changes to be made to mitigate risks and address issues before they become out of hand or too expensive to fix.

Kappelman's research into the driving forces behind risk defines a combination of "people factors" and "process factors" (these were further validated by industry studies on complex projects conducted by the PMI in 2012). Collecting the data necessary for monitoring risk can be done systematically, by asking project stakeholders (management, staff, and customers) a series of questions that address key factors periodically during the project. Typically, a weekly questionnaire, administered via email, proves sufficient to capture information necessary for dashboards.

Monitoring these key human factors is certainly efficient, and the results, as we've seen, are effective. But how do organizations address the issue of noncompliance? What if questionnaires are ignored? The fuel of the predictive engine runs on data (the more, the better). In an era where professionals are bombarded with daily electronic reminders, offers, and solicitations, developing a strategy to keep the source of information flowing is critically important.

Some organizations that we've worked with are successful at making responses a condition of employment, effectively mandating high participation levels. Some appeal to logic (it's less burdensome on an employee to answer a standard set of 15 multiple-choice questions than attend a 2-hour status meeting!) A sustained and methodical approach, incorporating best practices for change management, is the most reliable. A typical three-phase approach includes preparing for change, managing change, and reinforcing change. Preparation of stakeholders and project participants typically involves education about the benefits and clear communication of expectations. The types of questions that must be addressed include the following:

- Why are we making this change? (What are the risk avoidance benefits?)
- Who is impacted by this new approach, and in what ways?
- Who can sponsor this initiative to drive success?

In short, to exploit the advantages that analytics brings, members of the organization must change how they do their jobs. Success will depend upon whether individuals (staff and management) embrace and learn a new way of working.

PROJECT RISK MITIGATION THROUGH DATA ANALYTICS

Collecting data pertaining to the EWS for continual analysis throughout a project dramatically increases the probability of successful project outcomes. The earlier in the project that this information collection begins, the more effective it will be in avoiding failure. Moreover, if failure is inevitable due to factors outside management's ability to control them, continual monitoring of EWS and analysis of results will identify those situations before they become costly disasters.

What Can Analytics Address?

Data collected by projects fall into the below-mentioned categories:

- The past (reporting on results of earlier activity)
- The present (real-time alerts about conditions that meet specific criteria)
- The future (prediction based on extrapolated values collected over time)

Let's examine each of these in detail. Current information (including real-time data and data from the immediate past, i.e., within the last 24 hours) is used for triggering status conditions that need immediate attention. The value of historical (extended past) data collected across projects is useful from an analytics perspective when it is used as a foundation for improvement, or for crisis management:

- As a window on current status and activity for key indicators across projects (measures of time, cost, and quality)
- To establish comparative benchmarks for performance (i.e., effort, quality) or risk factors as a means of addressing longer-term organizational issues.

The most effective use of these data is seen when they are used for post-project reviews and to create checklists of possible problems for future projects. These can be reviewed while planning new projects, as lessons learned, and as sources of early warning signs.

It's clear from our experience and the literature that assessments based on historical data are useful for adjusting processes and instituting improvement programs that can reduce environmental risk. Of greater value to overall quality and mitigation of failures, however, is data with predictive capability. Data supporting Kappelman's EWS, analyzed continuously, produces a window on a project's future directions.

Across the IT industry, the volume of data for analyzing predictive elements is steadily increasing. Crowdsourced opinions, social media, and the Internet as a source of real-time information are making available information at unprecedented levels. Analytics allow project managers better understanding of how every project fits into the overall environment, as well as its effects on each other. Whether the goal of a project is to increase quality, resolve a system problem, improve operations, or prevent losses, analytics provides managers and stakeholders the insight necessary to reduce risk and increase success.

Of course, it's important to apply and act on insights that come from this information. Obtaining meaningful insights has become more difficult at about the same rate as the increase in the volume of data. Automation and strategies for making meaningful decisions from "first order" data (past, present, and predicted future) are essential. In smaller organizations, senior managers may be able to provide the interpretation necessary to make appropriate decisions. But in today's world of complex, large-scale projects and portfolios, automation has become vital. The most powerful insights come from artificial intelligence (AI)-based systems that have the ability to evaluate conditions and trends, anticipate effects, and recommend or execute specific actions to mitigate evolving risks.

Within an IT organization, each key role can benefit from the use of data analytics. Table 8.2 identifies key benefits of the information contained in a typical governance support system for the CIO, IT managers, directors of the project management office, and project managers.

TABLE 8.2

Analytics Use by Organizational Audience

CIO or Senior IT Management	IT Managers	Project Management Office	Project Managers
Continuously monitor the health and status of projects	Catch potential project risks before they become problems	Ensure consistency in processes and best practices across the organization	Monitor the health status of every project dimension
• Obtain visibility into project health and status • Align IT resources with business needs • Ensure compliance with industry best practices	• Manage by walking around virtually • Build productive project teams • Ensure projects are meeting business needs	• Ensure industry standards are applied to every project • Develop a culture of learning and growth	• Manage the human dimensions of projects • Receive early warnings of trouble • Dramatically reduce time spent in meetings

Online System for Visibility and Control

Computer Aid, Inc. developed a system that makes use of Kappelman's research to collect data about EWS and other critical measures. The automated project office (APO) system, which operates in the Cloud, collects both operational hard data and qualitative human feedback data across projects, throughout the life cycle (Figure 8.3).

The APO analytics engine produces dashboard views across projects in an organization, comprising both historical trends and indicators of the current and future status. Red, yellow, and green colors indicate status. Users can drill down to individual projects, or examine source data yielding a particular result. Managers and key stakeholders can, at a glance, identify areas of concern and downward trends in key process indicators (KPIs) and for the specific, EWS values (Figure 8.4).

Other dashboards provide visual cues on specific EWS indicators. In addition, since the system imports operational hard data from project management, issue management, and time recording tools, a variety of comparative measures can be observed, for individual projects and across collections of efforts (Figure 8.5).

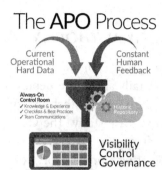

FIGURE 8.3
The APO process.

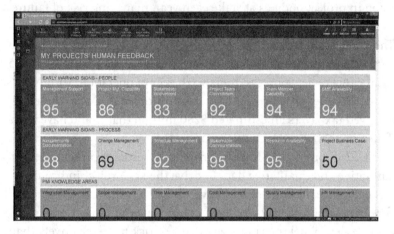

FIGURE 8.4
APO human feedback summary dashboard.

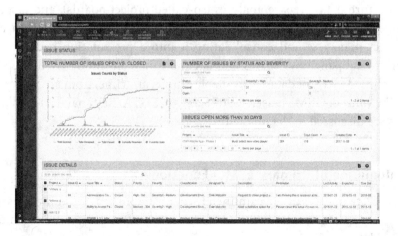

FIGURE 8.5
APO issues by status detail dashboard.

CASE EXAMPLE: GEORGIA TECHNOLOGY AUTHORITY

In his recent book, *The Strategic CIO: Changing the Dynamics of the Business Enterprise*, Phil Weinzimer provides details about the deployment of an enterprise governance system by the Georgia Technology Authority (GTA). Following is a summary of that case study. The GTA handles IT services and operations for the state of Georgia. The GTA saves taxpayer money across 119 state agencies by operating a process for project evaluation, review, governance, and tracking. With as much as $450 million in project budgets at stake each year, managing risk of failure and maintaining control is a priority.

The GTA implemented the APO system in 2012 as an integral part of Georgia's enterprise management suite (GEMS), automating the Georgia critical panel review process. In its sixth year of operation, with APO supporting the enterprise project management office (EPMO), these reviews have saved taxpayers an estimated $280 million that would have been lost to failed or challenged technology projects.

The GEMS project dashboard provides a visual representation of the quantitative and qualitative data to drive the key project indicator gauges to reflect ranges within red, yellow, or green, a benefit they never had before. Knowing the range of each color helps the project managers and critical review panel interpret the degree of risk more effectively than the previous process.

Prior to implementing GEMS, the GTA's greatest challenge was the time to capture data, prepare analyses (so-called project boards), and display project status. The manual process of collecting project data from the project managers and consolidating it into a presentation package for the critical panel review was manual and time-consuming. With GEMS, dashboard views of data are available online, any time, from anywhere.

The value of GEMS is seen today across the GTA. Key analytics capabilities are discussed in the following.

Automation of Primary EPMO Functions

- Data updates are streamlined through automated questionnaires for human factors and API connections to source project management data.
- Projects are evaluated from several project roles.

- Dashboards showing key process indicators are driven by combined qualitative and quantitative data.
- Issue tracking automates the reporting, resolving, and closing of issues.
- Communication is facilitated across the organization on risk factors and emerging issues.
- Gate questionnaires enhance process compliance.

Analytics Data Gathering

In many organizations, a major challenge is the effort required to capture data, prepare project dashboards, and display project status. What previously required more than 80 person-hours (to manually collect and consolidate project data for the critical panel review) now takes only about 4 hours.

Predictive Analysis

A set of algorithms based upon assessment data is used to derive solutions for predictive analysis. These are used to predict potential risks for key projects and across the portfolio of systems. This capability makes the solution a proactive process of anticipating risk and mitigating actions prior to the risks occurring.

Implementation Challenges Addressed

GEMS addresses a number of issues that have in the past made it difficult for GTA to obtain value from data as shown in Table 8.3.

Applied Data Analytics: Required Capabilities

In order to use data analytics to improve project management and governance in IT, the following critical capabilities are required. The set of functions a system must provide to support decision-making include the following:

1. Governance for a portfolio of projects across an organization.
2. Ease of implementation and simplicity of operation, with a high cost–benefit ratio.

TABLE 8.3

Challenges vs. Resolutions

Challenge	Resolution
Time-consuming and unreliable project data collection across projects and locations	Now streamlined and automated through the APO system
Project status data	Now made actionable with human feedback from key stakeholders
Access to information across units is cumbersome and/or costly	Now made transparent with an integrated, Cloud-based platform
Risk assessment limited to analysis of completed activities	Now enhanced with predictive project behavior, synthesized from early warning sign ratings
Inadequate issue management capability limits perspective of risks by management	Issue tracking system, integrated with project dashboard

3. Web or Cloud-based distributed solution, giving access to anyone, anywhere, and at any time.
4. Capture of qualitative, human feedback data from stakeholders.
5. Ease of access (importing) for project data: financials, resources, effort, and tasks.
6. Issue management for tracking through to resolution.
7. Identification of key risk indicators and predictive risk scores based on qualitative and quantitative data.
8. Learning and feedback to improve the skills of project managers.
9. Dashboard graphical views of data and measures.
10. Facilitated capture and analysis of critical project data, including investment parameters.

Key Implementation Challenges

The promise of data analytics brings the power of "crowdsourced opinions"—asking many people to answer the same questions about project status and KPIs—to bear on the problem of project risk. This approach provides a more accurate representation than obtaining reports from a few project insiders or the project manager. Automated collection of human feedback is more effective than verbal reports in public forums, such as meetings with managers. Analytics resulting from the "360-degree view" afforded by online tools are more reliable than simply expressed opinions.

This facilitates risk mitigation by enabling prediction of issues before they become impossible to control.

When KPIs are monitored in a one-stop shop containing quantitative and qualitative "human feedback" data, they facilitate regulatory oversight and compliance with governance, regulations, and policies. The concept of a virtual, online control room for monitoring and mitigating risk has tremendous potential value. Despite the benefits, organizational resistance can develop as a reaction to changes in reporting methods and complacency can be a challenge and must be managed carefully.

Unless organizations manage change effectively, achieving the full benefits of a transition to using data is difficult. What does it take to implement an effective set of analytics to improve governance? Areas of concern (and opportunities for change management practice) focus on the following:

- *Leadership*: Engaged executive sponsors must clearly define the anticipated benefits, establish chains of command, set clear objectives for success, and communicate results across the organization.
- *Acknowledgment of limitations*: Data analytics alone cannot replace the need for executive insight or decision-making. Implementation of processes and tools to increase organizational success depends on leadership and direction for future enhancement.
- *Measurement and reporting*: Results and continuing benefits must be communicated across the organization (participants, stakeholders, and management).

BEYOND TODAY'S ANALYTICS

The state of the art in project risk mitigation uses data analytics to highlight management insights and steer decisions. When implemented in an automated tool, managers obtain unprecedented visibility about results and trends for future unknowns. By balancing performance and quality analyses, these systems provide organizations with an accurate picture of risks and anticipated bumps in the road.

Existing tools, combined with consultative change management, address the primary concerns and challenges of implementing data analytics solutions, but there is room for improvement in how the analytics are used in organizations. Once a base of data is accumulated and the mechanics are in place to continuously feed it, the next step is to automate the application of knowledge to the environment. Advances in AI can be used to further leverage the data. Instead of simply reflecting business performance, data analytics can become the driver of operations.

The technology to automate actions based on observations (red flags, downward trends, etc.) with a minimum of human intervention exists today. Models for applying AI to analytics are found in IT operational monitoring and control systems. In the realm of DevOps and infrastructure management, artificial intelligence operations (AIOps) technology has taken the lead in interpretive controls for networks and computer hardware. Industry leading solutions use event "watchers" that identify trends (e.g., in disk arrays) that signal near-term failures. In industrial businesses, supervisory control and data acquisition (SCADA) systems perform monitoring and process controls.

Recently, AI-based robotic systems that automate SCADA across locations and platforms have assumed responsibility for formerly human tasks to adjust controls. Likewise, the future of data analytics for project management is in proactive detection and repair, using AI for machine learning, adaptive process control, and automated workflow across teams and tools.

The future of data analytics in the realm of project management lies in the way that business process automation is applied. Robotic process automation (RPA) is an emerging form of clerical process automation technology based on the notion of software robots or AI workers. A variety of open platform, highly configurable tools using RPA have been introduced into the market since 2014. Designed to perform repetitive tasks, software robots interpret, trigger responses, and communicate with downstream systems. The advantages of business process automation (as compared to using human analysts) with these robots include:

- Ease of "training" through simple, parameter-controlled interfaces (obviating the need for programming)
- Ease of integration with enterprise systems, dashboards, and management control tools
- Rapid and exhaustive data collection (24/7 across time zones) provides insights for ongoing business enhancement
- Continuous monitoring and availability of status reports through logs and management dashboards

TABLE 8.4

Evolution and Future of AI Process Automation

	Application-Specific Workflow Automation	Robotic Process Automation	Cognitive Robotics	Intelligent Robotics
Era	2000	2010	2014	2016→
Increase in Efficiency	5–20%	40%+	60%+	80%+
Characteristics	• Rule-based • Scripts and macros • APIs	• Cross-application • System-wide workflows • Complex rules • Process automation • Automation of user activities	• Integrated with cognitive services • Image integration • Natural language processing • Voice recognition • Virtual assistants	• Self-learning • Deep learning • No or low-code training • Natural language generation • AI screen recognition

Today, the spectrum of capability in the use of data for control and optimization of projects runs from basic AI to extended intelligent automation. Table 8.4 shows characteristics of technologies from early workflow systems to present-day cognitive intelligence-driven controls. The first attempts to automate processes focused on specific applications and were based on simple rules. With the advent of RPA, tools are able to operate across business applications and global networks, executing complex, multipath rules. Cognitive RPA adds a dimension of intelligent decision-making, as well as multimedia input (voice and vision control). With integrated deep learning capability, the latest intelligent robotics technology can automate the end-to-end learning. The implications for project control and governance is that the system can ask the right questions as well as provide appropriate answers.

The intelligent control room has arrived. With the inception of cognitive-intelligent robotics systems combined with rich data, fully interactive decision-making systems are becoming the state of the art. Cost-effective solutions for automating end-to-end management of complex projects, guided by data analytics, are within range of most project management organizations.

9

Conventional and Unconventional Data Mining for Better Decision-Making

Klas Skogmar

CONTENTS

You may have heard about data mining and may think about it as an IT-supported analysis of data in organizations. In the context of this chapter, however, data mining refers to the selection, refinement, and analysis of data to make decisions or resolve some type of problems. In that sense, all projects need to work with data mining. It may be to provide the project sponsor with the proper decision support, to manage stakeholder expectations, or to ensure proper estimates from the project team. In this chapter, some traditional techniques for data mining will be analyzed in a project context, as well as some unconventional ways that data can be mined, and used, to maximize project success.

WHY INFORMED DECISIONS ARE IMPORTANT

Decisions are a critical part of every project. Every day team members need to make decisions about their work, the project manager about how to act on that work, the project board approves project documents, program managers decide on the prioritizations of projects, and the portfolio decides the proper resource allocations to optimize the portfolio. These decisions are reactions to events that befall us and affect the outcome as well as future events. Understanding that decisions are made at all levels is important, as it also means that everyone involved in a project need to understand how they can make good decisions to maximize the likelihood of project success.

Decisions are made already before a project is being started, when project portfolio management evaluates a business case to decide if a project should be started or not. This is often referred to as "doing the right thing," as opposed to the decisions to optimize ongoing projects which in contrast is about "doing things right." Portfolio management in this context is what connects the organization's strategy to the execution, and thus project decisions influence both the efficiency and effectiveness of the future organization.

Making the right decisions can determine if a project, and the resulting outcomes and benefits, becomes a success instead of a failure, while bad decisions can set the wrong expectations on stakeholders, could make the project team run in different directions, or just let an unjustified project continue.

An infamous example of a project where a critical decision influenced the outcome is NASA's Challenger project, where the warnings from technicians about the influences of the extremely cold weather at time of launch were ignored and then the spacecraft exploded just a minute into its flight, killing all the seven crew members. It has been determined that the decision-making process was at fault. The decision-makers ignored recommendations and made the decision to launch without data to support it. NASA senior manager, Jud Lovingood, said, "You don't do data by emotion."* They did not have the proper data, and they knew it, but they still made a decision, which, in hindsight, proved to have catastrophic consequences.

This chapter will try to go through some of the things you can do to avoid such failures.

WHAT CAUSES BAD DECISIONS?

To be able to determine how to make good decisions, it is critical to first know the causes of bad decisions. Some of the most important aspects of bad decisions are:

1. Biases
2. Bad data
3. Wrong data
4. Too much data
5. Not using the data

There are other aspects, such as the decision-making process and the culture of an organization, but this chapter will focus on the use of (or lack of using) data. Let's have a look at each of these causes.

Biases

Biases are systematic errors in how humans perceive things and make decisions. Biases influences how we search for information (e.g., confirmation bias), how we interpret information (e.g., the framing effect), how me make decisions (e.g., sunk cost fallacy), or how we look back at past decisions (e.g., hindsight bias).

---

* www.nasaspaceflight.com/2007/01/remembering-the-mistakes-of-challenger/.

Biases are unconscious, which means that we make these systematic errors without being aware of them. We try to find data that justify our decisions, make decisions based on our belief systems, and take credit for successes and blame failures on others. To cope with biases we need to make ourselves aware of them and ensure we compensate for them.

Over the last two decades there has been a lot of research into different kinds of biases, and there are plenty of peer-reviewed studies published on the subject. We will look at a few of them related to the topic of data mining.

Confirmation Bias

Confirmation bias is the tendency for people to search, use, and interpret only the type of information that supports their existing beliefs. In decision-making this means it is likely that decision-makers will focus on only one alternative when making decisions, reducing the likelihood that it will be a good decision.

Framing Effect

Depending on how you look at a decision and how you frame it, the decision will be different. A threat can be framed as an opportunity, which makes the decision-maker become more innovative, or a collection of products may be perceived better when there are no defective parts, even if the collection in other ways is better than the alternatives. The framing effect has been proved in research and practice and is important to remember in a project context, as communication about the project (and thus the framing) is one of the key things that can be influenced by a project manager when it comes to the major decisions of the project.

Sunk Cost Fallacy

The sunk cost fallacy is when people increase support for a decision that has been previously made, as the investments accumulate, even though new data proves the previous decision to be wrong.

Hindsight Bias

Hindsight bias is the "I told you so" bias. When looking back at past decisions or advice, you will more easily remember those that proved to be correct than those that were wrong. In fact, your memory will actually be adjusted in your mind to make the historical data you perceived better by yourself. In a project context, there will be a lot of people who "knew" how the project would end already from the start, no matter if it turned out to be a failure or success.

Optimism Bias

Optimism is our inherent tendency to overvalue reward and undervalue risk and/or effort. Most of the time, the things we do takes longer to achieve and yields less than we have planned and hoped for. There is no exact optimism factor that we can determine, either for individuals or groups. But we do know that a vast majority of people exhibit optimism most of the time, and some of us are chronic pessimists. Pessimism is just optimism in reverse, the tendency to undervalue reward and overvalue risk and effort.

Overconfidence Bias

Overconfidence is our tendency to overstate our certainty in our estimates. We tend to believe we are much more certain than we are. We are especially bad at estimating certainties near 0% or 100%, since we tend to overestimate the occurrence of the very unlikely. So not only do we make claims that we can deliver a lot more at lower cost than we should, but we are also convinced that we are certain in those estimates. This is also known as expert bias as you are more vulnerable to is the more of an expert you are on the topic at hand.

Anchoring Bias

Anchoring is a bias that makes us "anchor" toward existing numbers when providing estimates of our own. The numbers could be totally unrelated, such as data given on a whiteboard in front of you, but in a project setting, early estimates are typical triggers of this bias. It is hard for someone to free oneself from an estimate done by someone else, even if that first estimate was widely optimistic.

Group Think

There are also a couple of biases that work on a group level. As social animals, we tend to be influenced by others when working in groups. One of these biases is called "group think," which makes us do what others are doing. If several other people are doing something, even if it by itself would be a strange behavior, it is likely that you will mirror the others, no matter if it is about what is being said, body language, or symbols used. This bias is particularly important when making decisions in a committee, as everyone in the group will be influenced by the others, and often people used to voicing their opinions loudly and with confidence will have more influence over the group than may be optimal for the decision.

How to Cope with Biases

To minimize the effect of biases, it is important to be aware of them, and that they apply to everyone. There is actually also a kind of "bias bias," which makes people believe biases apply to others, but not oneself. When biases have been acknowledged, there need to be motivation to correct for the biases. A part of this could be understanding the consequences of not correcting for biases, but when it comes to correcting for deeply entrenched beliefs or values, it may be hard to become motivated. In an organization, or within a project, it may be possible to motivate people as a group through a culture of transparency and correctness. It may also be possible to use some of the techniques in Cialdini's "influencing," such as asking people to make minor commitments before moving to greater commitments. When there is motivation, the amount of adjustment needs to be understood, so that the correction for the existing bias can be implemented. It should also be noted that for some biases, such as group think, there are valuable techniques to be applied, such as the Delphi technique, which is also described in PMI's PMBOK® Guide. To remedy the hindsight bias, it can be useful to document and agree on the definition of, and criteria for, success with major stakeholders.

An interesting way of reducing overconfidence in estimates is to use techniques outlined in Douglas Hubbard's *How to Measure Anything*. You can train people in estimating uncertainties, by asking people to repeatedly to test, asking for estimates of things where there is a known answer. An example could be to provide the 90% confidence interval of the height of the Eiffel tower. People should on average get 90% correct answers if they are "calibrated," but more common in initial tests is to get around 40% correct answers. After some time most people will actually be calibrated after doing several of these tests, in as little as 3–4 hours of training. This calibration training will then stick with them and make these people better in estimating uncertainty than others.

To cope with the sunk cost dilemma, it is vital to always have business cases that reflect the future, discarding the "sunk costs," but at the same time considers historical failures repeatedly as an indication of a failing ability of providing estimates, and acknowledges that it is likely that revised estimates most likely are influenced by biases, such as anchoring. To remedy this, it is critical to have proper estimates early, clear criteria for terminating a project (to avoid attachment to any previous decision to start a project), and to ensure revisions of estimates are done by calibrated estimators that are not influenced by previous estimates.

Bad Data

Another problem when making decisions is the quality of the underlying data. Sometimes measurements are unreliable. If the data is incorrect, any decision will be based on the wrong assumptions. Examples of this category in a project context could be subjective estimates that are influenced by biases, or there may issues with historical data that will be used for risk assessments. Even status reports from project managers to their sponsors, where they tell the status of using "subjective" evaluations, such as red, green, and amber values for certain dimensions of the project fits into this category. It is not uncommon for project managers to lie to make the project look better on paper than in reality, especially in organizations where the project manager's performance is evaluated based on project success.

Wrong Data

Having the wrong data is another common cause of bad decisions. This also includes situations where you don't have enough data (such as in the Challenger example in the Introduction), where you have the wrong focus or a just a lack of technical depth. The reason why some people collect the wrong data may be a version of the confirmation bias mentioned before. It makes people try to justify their position and beliefs, rather than trying to disprove it.

Too Much Data

Sometimes it can be problematic to have too much data. Even if the correct data is there it is not possible to find the relevant bits or to find patterns in the data. The challenge is like finding a needle in a haystack. The challenge

158 • *Data Analytics in Project Management*

of finding the proper patterns in large amounts of data is sometimes referred to as "big data" and may require looking at the data from many different perspectives to ensure that the right conclusions can be made. Sometimes biases, such as the confirmation bias, will influence the search for patterns or the insights made, which is a particular risk when there is a lot of data, as statistics can often be tweaked to make certain conclusions seem more relevant than they are. Therefore it is also important to try to disprove any hypothesis you may have with the data available. A specific person can be appointed to play the devil's advocate, which enhances the likelihood of incorporating multiple perspectives. When looking at big data, it is useful to have a good understanding of statistics. It is better to ensure that the easiest way of looking at the data is chosen, for example just using the mean because that is most common, where in some situations it is preferable to look at the median (e.g., because 50% of all measurements are below the median, which is not the case for the mean). Graphical representations is also a good way of analyzing large sets of data, and there are a lot of tools available to easily visualize the data from multiple perspectives, such as QlikView.

Not Using the Data

Finally, one problem that may occur is that data may be ignored. It may happen during the data mining itself, for example discarding certain data sources just because the data is complicated to get hold of, or even ignoring the analysis made through data mining, because someone believes that their gut feeling outperforms any data collected. This disbelief in facts is quite common and can be hard to overcome, since some people believe that their decision style does not rely on data, and then it can be hard to convince them to do it differently, especially if the argumentation is fact based.

Sometimes data may not be used to to make decisions, because the data gathered does not actually provide any insights into the decision to be made or problem to be solved. This may occur if the wrong assumptions have been made.

In some cases, even when the right data is there, and the correct decision seems obvious, the decision may still never be made. This could be indecisiveness of the decision-makers, or the lack of energy due to "decision fatigue" as decisions require willpower to be made.*

---

* *Willpower* by Baumeister.

HOW TO MAKE GOOD DECISIONS

"Making good decisions involves hard work. Important decisions are made in the face of great uncertainty, and often under time pressure."*

In order for decisions to be as beneficial as possible to our stated goals, we need to make sure that they are grounded in knowledge rather than gut instinct. A common misstep is to default back to personal biases and beliefs (a.k.a. gut instinct) when there is an apparent lack of facts to support a decision; however, there is usually plenty of information that will render valuable knowledge about what those facts could possibly and plausibly be.

If you follow these three steps, you will considerably improve the way you make your decisions:

1. *Decide how to decide.* For improved decisions, as well as better stakeholder support for those decisions, the process for making decisions should be clear to everyone involved. The accountability and mandate of decision committees should be clear. Are the decisions made through majority votes? Do we allow "gut feeling" or should the decisions be strictly formal? What type of input for the decisions will be required? Who will provide input?
2. *Decide what and when to decide.* Should certain types of decisions be delegated, and how does escalations look like? Should there be a tollgate model for project decisions, and what decisions should be taken, and by whom?
3. *Ensure proper decision support.* To ensure proper decisions, the input for the decision support materials should be of high quality. Knowledge and information should come from the proper data sources and analysis techniques. Ensure that people who provide input are the right people, with the right skills and insights (Figure 9.1).

These steps may seem simple enough, but a lot of things needs to be considered to do it right, such as minimizing bias and do proper data mining as outlined in this chapter. Use facts rather than emotions.

Another way of improving decisions is to use "wisdom of the crowds." Many people can in general outperform experts, if those people are diverse (representing many different viewpoints), and if they are anonymous

---

* https://hbr.org/2017/03/root-out-bias-from-your-decision-making-process.

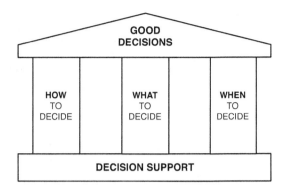

FIGURE 9.1
The pillars of good decisions.

(avoiding group think). This has been described in detail in the book *The Wisdom of the Crowds.**

WHY DATA MINING IS NEEDED

As we have seen, wrong data, bad data, or too much data are common causes of decisions, and often our collection of data and the interpretation are influenced by our biases. To counter this we need to ensure that we collect the proper amount of data, process the data, and analyze it in the best way possible. It is this quest to find patterns and knowledge that is at the core of data mining. Although data mining will have varying definitions, we will define it broadly to encompass aspects of domains such as business intelligence, big data, data analytics, statistical analysis, and machine learning, but where there is a specific goal to be achieved. Data mining helps us make informed assumptions about facts we do not know at the present.

HOW DO YOU DO DATA MINING

There are many variations described on how to do data mining, and even other measurement-centric methods originating from, for example, Six Sigma, who used the process of DMAIC: define, measure, analyze, improve, and control. Here is a simplified version that contains four different steps (Figure 9.2).

---

* *The Wisdom of Crowds* by James Surowiecki.

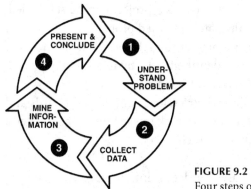

FIGURE 9.2
Four steps of data mining.

It is presented as a circular, repeating process, as many times, you will need to repeat the process as insights gained about a problem may alter the problem definition. This also aligns well with Deming's plan, do, check, and act process.

Understand the Problem or Decision

To be able to do good data mining, it is vital to be able to describe the problem to be solved or the decision to be made. If data is just collected to make sense of it, it will take a lot of time and effort to come to any conclusion. This may be fine for research, but working with projects, programs, or portfolios, the time aspect is often critical, and therefore there should always be an underlying need that the data mining should try to resolve. The description of the needs for data mining should be agreed with relevant stakeholders and documented publicly. Depending on the organization and project, the efforts for this work may vary, but it can, in some situations, be a considerable part of the work required.

As soon as the need has been agreed upon, it is also good to establish the process. Establish how, when, and by whom data will be collected, mined, and presented. Also decide how the results should be used, and if it will be input to a decision, describe how the decision will be made.

Examples of traditional uses for data mining in a project, program, and portfolio context are as follows:

- *Management reports*, enabling important stakeholders to control a project. Data may be collected to ensure the business case is still valid, or by using earned value management metrics to show progress compared to plan.

- *Time and cost estimates*, which ensures a project can be scheduled, budgeted, resourced, and ultimately planned properly.
- *Risk analysis*, which enables a project to make better assessments of the probabilities and risks of identified risks by including historical data, multiple perspectives, and unbiased estimates.
- *Project, program, and portfolio metrics*, for example dashboards and KPIs, allowing the project to stay on track toward the success criteria defined, while involving major stakeholders.

There are of course many other uses for data mining in projects, and the above examples are provided just to give a sense of the potential widespread use of data mining within this domain.

Collect the Data

When the purpose of the data mining is well understood, it is time to collect data. To achieve this, data sources need to be found, data need to be explored, cleaned, integrated, and preprocessed as much as possible to enable proper analysis.

Sources of data could be people, databases, files and file archives, IT systems, or published historical performance data. When collecting data from people, it is important to be aware of the biases mentioned earlier. To ensure data sources are not being missed, it can be a good idea to have a brainstorming session with some key resources. If the project has a list of stakeholders, then that list can be a good input to such a workshop, but the workshop should ensure that other types of resources are also considered.

To collect the data, there are many different ways, such as surveys, structured interviews, getting access to systems, going through previous project data, or even using web searches. There are also anonymized techniques, such as the Delphi technique, to ensure that input from experts are not tainted by group think.

No matter the technique applied, it is important to understand that as soon as people are involved, there may be resistance, as collecting data may be perceived as controlling people, not trusting them. Therefore, knowing the purpose of the data collection, and communicating this to everyone involved is crucial to get truthful and relevant data.

When doing research, the data sources selected should properly represent the average of the given domain, in the same manner as statistical analysis of, for example, voting patterns tries to ensure that a proper coverage of the population is being made. Depending on the problem or decision to make, this may be more or less important, but independently how well this has been done, it is important to understand the data sources not being selected (or responding in case of surveys). This enables the final analysis to adjust for the lack of data, or at least describe the shortfalls of the analysis itself.

When data has been collected, it may have to be integrated, if several data sources have been involved. It is common to use Excel for this, as there are many ways data can be stored and presented. Sometimes integration and cleaning of data can be a substantial part of all effort required to do data mining, depending on the organization, and the type of data collected.

Before doing analysis, sometimes the data also needs some preprocessing to be able to analyze the data. It could be to set up pivot tables that allows the analyzer to view the data from different perspectives, or it could be to enter the data into tools that can find patterns in the data, such as QlikView, RStudio, STATA, or Matlab.

Mine the Information

When data has been properly prepared for analysis, it is time to do the actual analysis. Now the data should be visualized, interpreted, and evaluated so that conclusions can be reached. This may require modeling, charts to be created, or calculating certain types of metrics to better understand the problem domain and finding potential answers or decisions to be made. Mining can be both structured, looking for specific data, or a form of discovery process to find input to the defined problem or decision. If a project should be started, for example, the business case is the most important document to make an informed decision. It is therefore vital, both that a business actually exists (which is not always the case), but also that the business case evaluates various options, to avoid many of the biases available. Also remember that the benefits may be hardest to measure, but also usually have the greatest impact on the business case, so a lot of analysis should be done there.

When working with lessons learned from historical projects, it is vital that the analysis acknowledges that each project is unique, while looking at trends and learnings that are applicable on a project level: do we constantly go over our time estimates? Are resources overused in certain parts our projects? Are there any key resources that seem to be bottlenecks in all projects?

There are many tools and techniques that can be used to make mine the data collected. Many originate from the field of statistics and are similar to techniques that have been used in research articles for a long time. Others are more about covering different perspectives, and others about finding patterns through visualizations. Three of these tools will be highlighted here:

- Regression analysis
- The AQAL model
- Charts and tables

Regression Analysis

One of the most useful tools for data mining is statistical regression analysis. It is a simple and well-known method that is extensively used in research and is being taught in all universities as part of their introductory statistics courses. Although it is outside the scope of this chapter to go through the details, the basics will be highlighted here. As an example, if the time of a project increases, so will the cost. Let's say that for a specific organization, there is a 10% delay in the project compared to schedule, but also a 15% overrun compared to budget. How much of this budget overrun is caused by the delay? What other factors are influencing? And how certain are we about the contribution from all the various parameters influencing?

Regression analysis enables you to look at the correlation between parameters. For example, if time increases by 10%, maybe the cost increases by 5%. If this is true for all situations, then, it is a perfect correlation. If it varies a lot, but there seems to be a pattern on average, then it is a weaker correlation. Regression analysis also enables you to evaluate this weakness and also enables you to do it for many variables in parallel. Although this is a strength of regression analysis, the more variables that you throw into the analysis, the higher is also the risk that you will find patterns that may be faulty. It just happens that the temperature correlates with the costs of the projects, which does not mean that there are any causalities there. The temperature is most likely not the cause of varying costs (although it cannot be excluded entirely, as weather in some projects actually could influence productivity). To get the best results, there should preferably be a list of candidate variables that you believe influence something and then try to look for patterns between those variables and the results.

TABLE 9.1

AQAL Analysis in Data Mining Context

	Internal	**External**
Individual	Subjective data, for example, through qualitative interviews. May have to be corrected for individual biases.	Objective data, for example, by measuring behavior. Bad data or not using the data are common issues.
Collective	Subjective data, but measured quantitatively, for example through surveys. Group biases should be considered.	Objective data on a collective level, for example the performance of processes. Too much data or wrong data are common issues.

The AQAL Model

A useful model to analyze anything is by using Ken Wilber's AQAL model. It ensures that the analysis takes both the internal as well as the external perspective, as well as looking at it from the individual and the collective. It is useful, as we through it can include subjective, objective, quantitative, and qualitative data by looking at it from different "lenses." If you look at decisions in a project context, the major influencing factors could be categorized like this (Table 9.1).

Through this model, it becomes easier to understand what type of data you are looking at, what additional types of data you can search for, as well as the types of issues that are most likely to occur during your data mining.

Charts and Tables

Charts are a powerful way of presenting data, as it allows us to visually see trends, patterns, or anomalies in data sets just by glancing at them. Instead of just providing the mean of a data set, showing the distribution in a graph will provide much more insights. In Six Sigma, graphs are frequently used to analyze data, for example using control charts, histograms, or Pareto charts.

Charts can also be used to show not only two dimensions, but three dimensions. An example is a graph type that is commonly used at the portfolio level, which is the bubble chart. In this chart, you can plot various projects, or project ideas, where each the axis represents, for example, value and risk, but where the size of the project (the "bubbles") represent the budget of the project. By looking at a chart like this, you can quickly

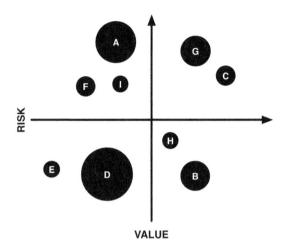

FIGURE 9.3

An example of a bubble chart, showing risk, value, and budget of projects.

see the projects that provides the most amount of value for the least amount of risk, but you can also get a feeling for the amount of resources required, and in some cases it may be better to have a high-risk project if it also could provide a lot of value (such as redirecting the business in a new direction) (Figure 9.3).

Tables may not be as intuitive as charts, but they usually make it easier to present exact data. Tables can also be useful as reporting tools but may need to be color coded or have additional information, such as trend arrows, making it easier to distinguish the relevant data from the rest.

Present and Conclude

When data have been collected, and insights have been made, it is important to package knowledge gained to convert it into a collective wisdom that can be used to make decisions and act. To be able to do this, it is important to be pedagogical, so that any insights made can be transferred to other relevant stakeholders. This is often best achieved by presenting results visually, but some unconventional methods could be to use storytelling or metaphors to make the point. Even though it is important to be pedagogical, it is equally important to not be too tainted by one's own preferences when presenting data to decision-makers. If one of the options seems better than the others, this underlying supporting data should form the basis of the argument. So while the data should not be tampered with, it should be noted that various stakeholders have different preferences in how they want communication. Some want details, whereas some want the holistic perspective. Some people prefer the facts, while others appeal to emotions. Ensuring that any presentation covers all communication preferences will increase the likelihood of everyone understanding the message.

As part of this last step, it should be noted that every decision and problem should lead to some actions. Without corresponding actions to change things, no decision will have any effect. As part of implementing a decision, the data mining can be used to gain support of major stakeholders.

After any decision has been made or a solution has been defined for a problem, more data mining should be done to verify the initial conclusions, as well as looking back to learn from the historical facts, to ensure future decisions are improved continuously.

UNCONVENTIONAL DATA MINING IN PROJECTS

Projects can use conventional data mining in various ways, but there are also some unconventional methods that can be used. There are situations where you might want to extend beyond the traditional data mining techniques to improve project success rates. One emerging best practice framework for entrepreneurial organizations is the lean startup.* It contains a structured process for ensuring the viability of a business idea, and contain three steps:

1. Build
2. Measure
3. Learn

When planning for this, however, it goes backward, so you should start by defining what you want to learn, then you should decide how you can measure that, and finally how you can build something that can deliver your measurements. Then you can start your steps by building, measuring, and learning. This is done iteratively, which ensures that you learn continuously. As you can see, the process is very similar to the data mining

---

* Lean Startup, Eric Ries.

outlined in this chapter, but there are some differences that needs to be highlighted. Lean startup is particularly useful for innovative projects or programs, for example within new product development, to continuously verify the business case. Lean startup ensures that verification of the business case is not focusing on the things that are easiest to measure, the costs, and puts more emphasis on the things that are most valuable to secure: the benefits. In a lean startup, an organization should have two hypotheses: a growth hypothesis and a value hypothesis. It can be useful to use these in business cases of organizations, which allows these hypotheses to be tested and reevaluated throughout a project.

Lean startup also describes how you can "pivot" from one idea to another, when it becomes apparent that there is no market for the original idea. This goes beyond the traditional go–no-go decisions, and instead tries to reuse created assets by reimagining the potential uses of what has been developed. This way of pivoting can be useful on a program level, where projects can be redefined to maximize the benefits.

Another unconventional way of using data mining is to reinforce or steer behavior. Eliyah Goldratt once said, "Tell me how you measure me, and I will tell you how I will behave." Although this is always important to be aware of when doing any measurements or data mining, so that any negative consequences can be avoided, it can also be used to reinforce positive behaviors. For a big national Swedish bus provider, an organizational change program had the goals of reinforcing new driving behaviors of all the bus drivers. Each bus had devices collecting data, which could then be gathered and presented in various forms. But instead of just presenting the resulting information to the management as a decision-making support, it was used to highlight the differences between the regions, and all data were reported to each regional manager, together with positive reinforcement of those that had performed well in the time period. This made it into a light hearted competition, where regions that had not performed well-contacted well-performing regions to learn from their experiences. As these measurements were not part of any reward systems, it promoted collaboration between regions, while still making improvements in all regions. No one want to look bad in a report, even if it does not influence your salary.

A final note on unconventional data mining is the rising use of machine learning methods, or "artificial intelligence" to aid decision-making. This is still not commonly used, but the methods are developing rapidly, new tools are made available and uses are being adopted in various fields.

Already machines can diagnose patients, analyze stock markets, and automatically detect people in images. This new development provides tremendous opportunities for development, also when making decisions in organizations and within projects, but there may also be some reasons for concerns, as we will then lack the ability to oversee and understand all parts of the decision-making process.

CONCLUSIONS

It is obvious that we take too many decisions based on emotions, where we instead should rely more on objective facts. Bad decisions are influenced by human biases, bad data, wrong data, too much data, and not using data being available. We can remedy this by making ourselves aware of our biases, and by having good data as input to our decisions, and data mining can provide that. We can adjust for biases by calibrating estimators, establish our decision at project startup, and use anonymous estimates from multiple people to avoid group bias and enable wisdom of the crowds.

To do data mining properly, it is critical to first understand the problem or decision, as without this guidance, it will be hard to collect the right type of data, and sometimes even the wrong conclusions can be drawn, as random correlations may suggest things that could be wrong. Therefore a lot of effort should be put to collect, clean, and transform data so that it can be analyzed properly. When mining data for information, statistical techniques should be considered, but also changing perspectives, for example through the AQAL model. As conclusions are drawn, it is critical to present and communicate these conclusions to various stakeholders in good ways.

Finally, some unconventional methods for data mining can be used in projects, programs, and portfolios, for example "lean startup," to drive desirable behaviors, or to use emerging technologies like artificial intelligence.

No matter how you will work with data mining in your projects, it is here to stay, as the amount of data and information is increasing exponentially, and there are no signs that it will decrease in the future. All domains will have to cope with this data, and it will be even more important that projects, introducing change in organizations and society, will be able to cope with this change themselves.

10

Agile Project Management and Data Analytics

Deanne Larson

CONTENTS

INTRODUCTION

Data mining is not a new capability and has been used in application since the early 1960s when statisticians attributed "data mining" as the name of the process for analyzing data for knowledge without a confirmed hypothesis (Mena, 2011). Within the last 10 years, the use of data mining has grown in scope to address the disruption of big data and the organizational need to stay competitive, resulting in the growing field of data analytics (Bole et al., 2015; Davenport, 2014, 2015; Halper, 2015; Sim, 2014). Data mining methodologies were introduced in 1996 with the introduction of Cross Industry Standard Process for Data Mining (CRISP-DM). Since that time, CRISP-DM remains the consistent methodology for data analytics projects. According to Gartner Research (2015), the stages of CRISP-DM are still relevant, but the methodology needs to be updated to address the challenges of data analytics project delivery. The increase in data volume, variety of new sources, and the speed at which data is available have made the use of traditional project management methodologies a challenge (Davenport, 2013). This same challenge was encountered by IT departments where pressure to deliver high-quality solutions faster demonstrated that waterfall project management methodologies were inadequate, which gave rise to agile project management methodologies.

Agile project management methodologies focus on the ability to respond to change using incremental and iterative practices. Agile as a practice was derived from software development (Aston, 2017). The manifesto and principles for agile software development (ASD) were published in 2001, and since then, the objectives and principles have been interpreted and applied to information technology (IT) project delivery. Beck et al. (2001) outlined the core values of the manifesto: individuals and interactions over processes and tools; working software over comprehensive documentation; customer collaboration over contract negotiation; and responding to change over following a plan. The result of following these values is that project delivery becomes less formal, more dynamic, and customer focused. Although some organizations may not classify data analytics projects as IT projects, these initiatives rely heavily on the need for information and technology to be successful (Davenport, 2013).

This chapter explores the application of agile methodologies and principles to data analytics project delivery. The objectives of this paper are threefold. First, explore the changing data landscape and prevailing methodologies. Second, analyze the alignment between agile values and principles to the goals of data analytics projects. Finally, propose agile project management methodology considerations and recommendations on managing data analytics projects.

THE CHANGING DATA LANDSCAPE

The increased use of Internet-connected smart devices has altered how organizations and individuals use information (Abbasi et al., 2016; Davenport, 2013; Halper, 2015). The Internet of Things (IoT), where data collection is embedded into devices, results in exponentially increasing amounts of data and contributes to the demand for fresher data. Monitoring equipment failures, for example, is now possible with data within seconds vs. data that takes hours or days to get (Halper, 2015). Exploring the change in the volume, variety, velocity, and veracity of data, otherwise known as the characteristics of big data, demonstrates the challenge in applying to traditional project management delivery methodologies.

Volume

Big data is pervasive in many industries including sports, health, retail, telecommunications, finance, manufacturing, technology, and security (Abbasi et al., 2016). The volume of data created used to be described in terabytes; however, terabytes have now been replaced with petabytes and exabytes. The growth of data impacts the scope of data used in projects. Scope increases project complexity where new technology is used to accommodate more data and more data results in increased data quality issues (Abbasi et al., 2016).

Variety

Data variety becomes a concern for project delivery as the types of data sources to be used for analysis increases. The variety of data means increasingly complex forms of data such as structured and unstructured data (Abbasi et al., 2016; Davenport, 2013; Halper, 2015). Transactional data, images, social network content, sensor data from IoT, rich text, and clickstream are all examples of the variety of data used in analysis. For instance, the analysis of images would require a translation of the image into an unstructured string of pixel coordinates. Additionally, data sources are not only valuable independently but also integrated, resulting in the need to integrate a variety of data structures. Both the translation and integration of data sources increase the complexity of projects.

Velocity

Velocity focuses on the speed of data creation. In 2014, Twitter, as an example, created one billion tweets on average every 3 days (Abbasi and Adjeroh, 2014). Data velocity challenges the ability to analyze trends and patterns. Historically, fresh data may have been categorized as data from the previous business day; but in the case of IoT, data that is an hour old may be too old for analysis (Halper, 2015). Data acquisition becomes a challenge as traditional data acquisition focused on extract, transformational, and load (ETL) of data. Increased velocity changes how data sources have been processed traditionally switching when data is analyzed and understood. With the increase in velocity, the data is loaded first and then analyzed promoting the use of NoSQL databases.

Veracity

Veracity deals with data accuracy. Projects that derive value and knowledge from data have always been challenged with credibility and reliability issues. Volume, variety, and velocity complicate this more and veracity problems increase. Understandability of unstructured data is a challenge as metadata does not exist and data completeness varies. The different types of sources complicates the veracity of data and the complexity of deriving knowledge from data increases (Abbasi et al., 2016; Davenport, 2013; Halper, 2015)

According to Mayer-Schönberger and Cukier (2013), big data changes how the world interacts and means a disruption to what was considered normal. This disruption also means disruption to the delivery of projects that derive knowledge and value from data. Big data results in changes to IT processes, technologies, and people. One greater reliance observed on data scientists need to address the complexity introduced with big data and help derive the knowledge from data (Abbasi et al., 2016; Davenport, 2013).

METHODOLOGY

Methodologies have value in that they help deliver projects effectively and efficiently, which, in turn, enables business value from the project investment (Grimes, 2006; Sim, 2014). Data analytics projects often are initiated without clear objectives and outcomes, inviting constant scrutiny on whether business value occurs (Larson & Chang, 2016). Deriving value from information means that each data analytics project needs to deliver usable results. Projects that result in useful information are complex, where each project is a transformational effort to create knowledge from data (Grimes, 2006). The scope of each data analytics project covers all activities that need to occur in the information value chain, which includes converting data into information and information into knowledge (Abbasi et al., 2016). Data analytics projects have increased in project complexity as converting information into knowledge requires the use of statistical and analytical models as well as incorporating the use of big data (Halper, 2015).

Sahu (2016) proposed that existing data mining methodologies need to be more dynamic in order to increase business value enabled from data analytics projects and that by adopting agile principles this could be possible. ASD has been applied to IT projects to deliver solutions faster with an intent on increasing business value (Aston, 2017). Alnoukari (2015) presented a methodology that leverages ASD principles and the CRISP-DM process called ASD-BI (Agile Software Development—Business Intelligence) supporting that both CRISP-DM and ASD can be combined to improve project delivery and business value. A detailed description and analysis of CRISP-DM and ASD values and principles follow.

CRISP-DM

CRISP-DM is a data mining process model that conceptually describes the stages that are used to tackle data mining problems. CRISP-DM was originally created to align with data mining but, it has organically evolved into the primary approach used by data scientists. CRISP-DM contains six stages that appear to be in sequence; however, the stages are not strictly sequential and iterating through the stages is expected (Marbán et al., 2009). The six stages are:

- Business understanding
- Data understanding
- Data preparation
- Modeling
- Evaluation
- Deployment

Business Understanding

Business understanding focuses on determining the business requirements and objectives to create a problem definition. Data analytics initiatives start with a question of interest or problem to be addressed. The outcome of this stage is a problem definition. The problem definition may be diagrammed using decision modeling or other approach (Marbán et al., 2009). Specific activities for this stage include the following:

- Determine business objectives
- Assess situation
- Determine data mining goals
- Produce project plan

Data Understanding

Once a problem statement is understood, data collection can proceed. Data collection involves obtaining data attributes required to address the problem statement. Often data integration is required as data may come from various sources in various formats. Once data is useable, data is profiled and statistically analyzed to determine demographics, relationships, distribution, and quality levels. The outcome of this stage is initial insights into the data to support the problem statement often referred to as exploratory data analysis (EDA) (Marbán et al., 2009). Specific activities for this stage include the following:

- Collect initial data
- Describe data
- Explore data
- Verify data quality

Data Preparation

Data preparation is necessary to create the data set that will be used in the analytical modeling stage. Data preparation includes the final integration of various attributes, cleansing of attributes, and deriving of new attributes. Activities in this stage are often iterative as new data may be required to support the subsequent modeling and evaluation stages. The outcome of data preparation is a data set that is to be used in the first iteration of modeling (Marbán et al., 2009). Specific activities for this stage include the following:

- Select data
- Clean data
- Construct data
- Integrate data
- Format data

Modeling

Various modeling techniques and algorithms are explored in this stage as there are several techniques that can be used to address one problem. The parameters of the analytical models are adjusted to improve model performance. It is possible to go back to the data preparation phase if additional data is needed or formatting needs to be adjusted (Marbán et al., 2009). Specific activities for this stage include the following:

- Select modeling techniques
- Generate test design
- Build model
- Assess model

Evaluation

Models are evaluated based on minimizing accuracy errors, bias, variance, and overall fit to the business objectives or problem statement. Before moving to deployment, a final review is completed to confirm the steps taken to create the model and then a final decision is made move to the deployment stage (Marbán et al., 2009). Specific activities for this stage include the following:

- Evaluate results
- Review process
- Determine next steps

Deployment

The model deployment scope will depend on the frequency of the model. Models can run one time, creating descriptive analytics or be a repeatable scoring model. Deployment to a production environment often occurs at this stage. Models are monitored to ensure quality, as model accuracy can degrade due to change and time (Marbán et al., 2009). Specific activities for this stage include the following:

- Plan deployment
- Plan monitoring and maintenance
- Produce final report
- Review project

The description provided of CRISP-DM is a summary and does not highlight the granularity of effort needed for successful data analytics outcomes. Many organizations use CRISP-DM as a framework and add steps to each stage for data analytics teams to follow. There was an effort to create CRISP-DM 2.0 in 2007, but there is no new research or activity in this area.

Agile Methodology

Keith (2006) recognized that agile methodology, although based on software development, can be applied more broadly to projects. Many agile methodologies have emerged since the agile manifesto was created in 2001. Methodologies such as Scrum, Kanban, Lean development, and extreme programming (XP) are examples and each share common properties of focusing on people and results through the use of collaboration and streamlined methods (Alnoukari, 2015). While there are benefits in each of these methodologies, the values and principles of agile development vs. the specific methodology is really the focus (Keith, 2006). Beck et al. (2001) created the values, as well as the principles listed below.

- Our highest priority is to satisfy the customer through early and continuous delivery of valuable software.
- Welcome changing requirements, even late in development. Agile processes harness change for the customer's competitive advantage.
- Deliver working software frequently, from a couple of weeks to a couple of months, with a preference to the shorter timescale.
- Business people and developers must work together daily throughout the project.
- Build projects around motivated individuals. Give them the environment and support they need, and trust them to get the job done.
- The most efficient and effective method of conveying information to and within a development team is face-to-face conversation.
- Working software is the primary measure of progress.
- Agile processes promote sustainable development. The sponsors, developers, and users should be able to maintain a constant pace indefinitely.
- Continuous attention to technical excellence and good design enhances agility.

- Simplicity—the art of maximizing the amount of work not done—is essential.
- The best architectures, requirements, and designs emerge from self-organizing teams.
- At regular intervals, the team reflects on how to become more effective, and then tunes and adjusts its behavior accordingly.

What is observed in the principles is that agile methodology means maximizing information flow between team members, thus reducing the time between decisions, and acting quickly on the results of the decisions for speed and flexibility. Agile is not rigid, but adaptable (Keith, 2006). Methodologies such as Scrum, Lean development, and XP are adaptive approaches, but use a plan–build–revise lifecycle. ASD is another agile method that embraces an adaptive approach, where plan–build–revise is replaced with speculate–collaborate–learn (Alnoukari, 2015). ASD demonstrates the applications of agile principles vs. a prescriptive methodology. Keith (2006) outlines that the phase of "plan" is too rigid, "build" is too process-focused, and "revise" does not address the learning that occurs in the process.

The agile movement has also produced agile project management, which focuses on scope flexibility, collaboration, and delivering quality results (Layton, 2017). Agile project management was also built on the agile principles and used Scrum as a framework, XP for a focus on quality, and lean development to reduce rework. Agile project management focuses on results, communication, people, and flexibility.

Agile Teams

Agile methodologies rely highly on specific team characteristics to be successful. Agile teams are small in size, typically seven team members as a target, and the entire team is accountable for delivery. The team is empowered and works autonomously as possible. Teams are collocated and each team member has a versatile skill set (Alnoukari, 2015). The three generic roles in an agile methodology are a project lead (sometimes referred to as a master), a product owner, and versatile team members who can assume many roles. The lead focuses on enabling the team success, while the product owner addresses stakeholder management, release management, and the backlog of requirements. Other project team members focus on the project deliverables.

GOALS OF DATA ANALYTICS

Data analytics is about finding insights from data; finding trends, behaviors, and inferences that enable organizations to make better business decisions (Lo, 2017). Organizations use data analytics based on the value it brings as it has been documented to decrease fraud, reduce customer and product churn, improve target marketing, identify new markets, improve operations, and increase profitability (Sim, 2014). For example, the U.S. retail organization Target uses data analytics to create customer segments based on shopping behavior and craft marketing campaigns to target these segments to increase revenue and maximize marketing spend. Another example is the online streaming and video-on-demand company Netflix. Netflix leverages content viewing patterns to determine what new content to produce. Netflix has evolved from a streaming service that streamed content created by others to a content creator, all based on the results of applying data analytics (Lo, 2017).

Ultimately, the goal of data analytics is to produce a data product, which is a technical asset that ingests data to return algorithmically generated results (Lo, 2017). An example would be a recommendation engine that tracks and ingests user's preferences and makes recommendations. Data products are designed to integrate into core business applications and processes to enable smarter business decisions at all levels.

Why the perspective of the data product? The concept of the data product provides a basis of why agile methodology principles should be combined with CRISP-DM processes. Keith (2006) outlined that working software is the measure of agile project success, but in data analytics, the working software is not valuable unless it provides business insight and better business decisions.

AGILE PRINCIPLES AND CRISP-DM

A review of ASD principles and CRISP-DM (as the primarily methodology for data analytics) demonstrates common characteristics. CRISP-DM has six stages that interact and iterate to the final stage of deployment (see Figure 10.1). The first stage of business understanding focuses on identifying the scope and success criteria; the second stage of data understanding identifies data sources and assesses each for quality; the third stage of data preparation phase involves identification of variables and cleaning the data; the fourth stage of modeling uses different analytics methods to analyze the data; the fifth focuses on evaluating the data product; and the sixth, the deployment stage incorporates the data product into regular use (Marbán et al., 2009). What is observed in five of the CRISP-DM stages is iteration and discovery, which will rely on a combination of business and technical collaboration, highlighting an alignment with agile values. According to Abbasi et al. (2016), CRISP-DM is analogous to the traditional software development lifecycle (SDLC) used in IT development. Agile methodologies were introduced to address some of the barriers of the traditional SDLC; thus it is logical to believe that CRISP-DM can also benefit from the benefits of agile values and principles.

The overall characteristics of CRISP-DM include the need to collaborate across multiple roles and disciplines within an organization and embrace change—two of the four ASD values. The high degree of collaboration also emphasized the use of the ASD value of individuals and interactions over process and tools. The last ASD value of working software also aligns with CRISP-DM as the outcome of the process is a working data product, which relies directly on working software. How both ASD values and the stages of CRISP-DM align are depicted in Table 10.1.

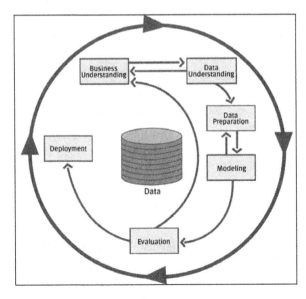

FIGURE 10.1
Demonstration of the iterative nature of CRISP-DM.

TABLE 10.1

Alignment of CRISP-DM and ASD Values

CRISP-DM Stage	ASD Value Alignment
Business understanding	Individuals and interactions over processes and tools; customer collaboration over contract negotiation
Data understanding	Individuals and interactions over processes and tools; customer collaboration over contract negotiation; responding to change over following a plan; working software over comprehensive documentation
Data preparation	Responding to change over following a plan; working software over comprehensive documentation
Modeling	Responding to change over following a plan; working software over comprehensive documentation
Evaluation	Customer collaboration over contract negotiation; responding to change over following a plan; working software over comprehensive documentation
Deployment	Working software over comprehensive documentation

Alignment

The alignment of ASD values and CRISP-DM begins with the uncertainty of scope. Data analytics is about exploring phenomena through observation and experimentation to obtain a deeper understanding. Which means the majority of data analytics initiatives occur with a high degree of uncertainty in the business understanding phase. Traditional IT project management approaches involve a high degree of planning with the goal of eliminating uncertainty. ASD focuses on uncertainty being a primary characteristic of the project, resulting in the ability to deal with change and opportunity.

Data analytics projects begin with a problem statement or question of interest tied to obtaining a particular business objective. The business and data understanding stages of CRISP-DM require close collaboration between technical and business resources, highlighting the need for customer collaboration. In order to identify the right data sources and business meaning there is less focus on process or tools. In fact, most data analytics projects use a multitude of tools to do the "data wrangling" needed to support data understanding and data preparation.

The stages of data understanding, data preparation, modeling, and evaluation are iterative due to data discovery and evaluation that happens in each of these phases. These CRISP-DM stages mimic the iterative design–development–test cycle that occurs in ASD, both of which highlight the need to respond to change and produce working software. Last, the evaluation and deployment stages support a working model vs. a focus on documentation.

ASD values are used to support the stages of CRISP-DM. CRISP-DM relies highly on collaboration, discovery (embracing change), and the delivery of working software. By leveraging the values of ASD, data analytics initiatives can take advantage of the most popular software delivery methodology in use today (Denning, 2015). Denning (2015) outlines that ASD is a key stepping stone for technical project delivery success.

APPLICATION OF AGILE VALUES

While the CRISP-DM process illustrates an alignment with ASD values, fundamental differences exist between the outcomes of ASD and data analytics. ASD is the default methodology used in software delivery and fully developed methodologies, such as Scrum and Kanban, where software is delivered in small increments. Applying ASD values directly to the data analytics process exposes gaps as data analytics is not only about delivering software but creating insights as outcomes of the process (Jurney, 2017). The commonality in outcomes between ASD and data analytics is working software; however, insight from data is not necessarily an outcome of ASD and is critical to the value of data analytics. Jurney (2017) proposes that the goal of agile data analytics is "to document and guide exploratory data analysis to discovery and follow the critical path to a compelling product" (p. 5).

Several challenges emerge with data analytics projects from the application of ASD methodologies such as Scrum and Kanban. Scrum is a highly used ASD framework that is based on cross-functional teams working in iterations within a time-boxed sprint. Kanban differs from Scrum in that it is less structured and focuses on incremental improvements. Kanban can be applied to any process, even Scrum, by managing work in progress (WIP). Kanban pulls work items (a.k.a. work packages, requirements, or stories) through the process focusing on optimizing the work flow of items (Jurney, 2017).

Challenges of ASD Applied to Data Analytics

Time-Boxing

Time-boxing means that time boundaries are placed around an activity. The time-box becomes a constraint that drives the team to focus on value or minimal viable product (MVP). One of the challenges that comes with using a time-boxed approach is that data analytics is a process that uses data to follow a chain of analysis. In this chain of analysis, it may not be clear what the next question is until the current question is answered. In addition, the next area of analysis may be clear, but there may be a dependency on gathering or acquiring more data. Given the primary outcome of actionable insights from data analytics, time-boxing does not promote iterative and progressive analysis.

Data Wrangling

Data wrangling is an umbrella term used to describe the process of acquiring, transforming, cleansing, and integrating data into one "raw" form that enables the consumption of data (Jurney, 2017). The CRISP-DM stages of data understanding and data preparation require multiple iterations of data wrangling before the modeling stage can begin. Data wrangling also pushes up against constraints of the time-box. ASD focuses on the client, the technical team, and the business but less value is placed on the data. In data analytics, all of the value is derived from the data.

Insight vs. Activity

In Scrum, work items will be assigned to a developer during a sprint, which results in software. Again, the focus with ASD is working software; however, working software may produce no insight. Without the insight, data analytics produces no value. Multiple iterations are needed to produce insight. Jurney (2017) refers to the multiple iterations in data analytics as concurrent experiments. ASD focuses on the completion of activity, where data analytics is focusing on actionable insights.

Quality, Testing, and MVP

In ASD, testing is a component of each development phase accomplished via constant feedback from those that determine the final product.

In data analytics, the "vision" of the final product is not typically known and quality is gauged on the insight derived. Quality in data analytics has different dimensions: software quality, model quality, and insights quality. Model quality is determined on accuracy rate and insights quality is based on creating new actions or improving existing ones. Accuracy rate may vary based on the initial problem. For instance, a 50% accuracy rate may be acceptable if the model addresses a problem never before addressed, thus an MVP version of a model may be acceptable. Acceptable software quality will depend on if the model is a one-time descriptive model or a model to be used in production scoring. Last, at the end of an ASD development cycle, the result is deployed and the team moves on to the next work item. In ASD, if insight quality is low, the data analytics team might work backward or skip back to steps in CRISP-DM to rework the model.

The challenges of ASD application to data analytics have a common root cause—uncertainty of how and when insights are considered valuable. A basic conflict exists between the experimental nature of data analytics and the framework of ASD. Iterative experiments produce learning where one experiment determines the next; there is no understood stopping point or final product.

DATA ANALYTICS AND BIG DATA

As outlined, big data has emerged due to the explosion of data—the types, the amounts, and the speed at which it is generated. The industry that is data analytics has evolved from the growth of data (Halper, 2016). Because of this quick evolution, often data analytics and big data are used interchangeably as if they are the same thing; however, they are very different. Data analytics, in several ways, is a result of big data, primarily due to the need to analyze data (other than traditional structured data) such as text, streaming, machine-generated, and geospatial data (Halper, 2016).

Impacts to Data Analytics Project Delivery

Technology Infrastructure

The impact of big data to data analytics project delivery can be observed in the technology infrastructure used. Traditional databases and servers are no longer sufficient to process multistructured disparate data sources. IT organizational infrastructures now include data lakes and NoSQL databases to acquire and land data sources (Halper, 2016). Analysis of big data requires the use of high-powered hardware such as in-memory processing and massively parallel processing (MPP) platforms, which support large amounts of data.

Open-source technologies can also be observed in the data analytics technology infrastructure. Three open-source technologies that have emerged include Hadoop, the statistical package R, and Spark. Hadoop is a framework that enables distributed processing of large data sets using commodity computer clusters and simple programming models (Halper, 2016). Hadoop scales quickly, which aligns well to big data. R is an open-source statistical language and environment used by many organizations to experiment with data analytics. R contains popular and current statistical algorithms. Spark is an in-memory processing framework that contains an analytics library and supports data streaming (Halper, 2016).

Multiple Skill Sets

The big data and data analytics infrastructure has become much more diverse and sophisticated, which highlights the need for deeper technical skills. The CRISP-DM stages of data understanding and data preparation often involve using specialized technical skills to acquire and ingest big data sources. Multiple technologies are involved in acquiring data from different sources in different formats and ingesting them for storage into data lakes—a data repository that holds large quantities of raw data in its original format for future needs (Halper, 2016).

Once data is acquired and ingested, multiple iterations are needed to analyze the data and prepare it for use in the modeling stage. Using R and Spark, for instance can play in the data understanding, data preparation, modeling, and evaluation stages. Data analytics is not often a single role or person with all of the required skill sets. Early data scientist job descriptions included advanced knowledge of statistics, math, computer science, and development as well as have a good understanding of industry and business. In addition, knowledge of machine learning methods and algorithms such as how they work and when to apply them is required. Having multiple skills sets is not an exclusive issue to big data, but it becomes more pronounced when using big data.

Technical Debt

Another by-product of the combination of big data and data analytics is technical debt—the extra work that arises when the development focus is on a model that works, but the process that goes into running the model is far from perfect (Jurney, 2017). Technical debt is highlighted more when big data is used in data analytics due to the increased complexity of the infrastructure used.

With ASD, code is the product, and thus quality is important. With data analytics, code tends to be discarded, so code quality is less important and the focus is on tolerating a lower degree of quality until insight and value emerge. Code in data analytics does not initially need to be perfect, but eventually will need to be of higher quality when a data product is ready for deployment.

Big data use in data analytics increases the technical complexity of data analytics projects. Multiple disparate technologies coupled with the use of open-source programming options and initial technical debt means the project leader will need to have a very diverse skill set to deliver value.

BEST PRACTICES IN DATA ANALYTICS PROJECT MANAGEMENT

Data analytics is still evolving, thus best practices are only starting to emerge. The following best practices have been synthesized from the author's experience as well as published best practices from leading analysts (Gartner, 2015; Halper, 2016; Larson & Chang, 2016).

Due Diligence in Defining Business Goals and Problem Statement

The success and value of a data analytics project is defined at the start of the project. Clearly defining the business goals to be addressed and formulating a problem statement will directly impact the CRISP-DM steps of data understanding and data preparation. If the investment is not made upfront to understand expectations, the subsequent stages in CRISP-DM will be impacted. Effort should be made to include the right stakeholders and determine any additional steps needed in the methodology.

CRISP-DM is a framework and detailed steps may need to be added to reflect the challenges in the organization. The problem statement should clearly identify the data needs of the project (Gartner, 2015; Halper, 2016; Larson & Chang, 2016).

Allow Time for Data Understanding, Acquisition, and Preparation

A key failure point in data analytics projects is planning enough time to get the data required for the project. Often the time needed to work with the data is underestimated or not known at the start of the project. Working with multiple technology platforms, multiple data structures, data sampling, data integration, and merging data into a final set for modeling takes time and planning. Additionally, once a final data set is created, the project team should document the data lineage to ensure the data processing logic is clear which can enable the recreating of the data set for iterative development (Gartner, 2015; Halper, 2016; Larson & Chang, 2016). Data lineage deals with the rawest form of data (data at its lowest grain), which enables efficiencies in data movement and storage resulting in higher return on investment in data analytics projects.

Identify Needed Toolsets and Skill Sets at Project Start

As outlined, the technology infrastructure in the data analytics industry can be varied and complex. Tools can be open source where support is lacking adding to the complexity. Technical tools are needed for analytical modeling and data wrangling, which are key for the success of the project. The project team will need to have a diverse set of roles focusing on technology, analytical modeling, statistics, and business skills. The project leader will need to have a strong technical and analytical skill set to lead the project. Identifying the tools and skillsets at project start prevents technical and team barriers during the iterative stages (Gartner, 2015; Halper, 2016; Larson & Chang, 2016).

Allow Time for the Cycle of Modeling and Evaluation

The value of data analytics occurs when insight is attained. Insight refers to the capabilities provided by the model, which typically falls in the categories of lowering risk, increasing revenue, increasing productivity, and supporting and shaping an organization's strategy (Larson & Change, 2016). Modeling and evaluation tends to be experimental, which results in answers, but also more questions. Models also need to be built with different algorithms to be able to validate accuracy increasing the time needed for more experimentation (Gartner, 2015; Halper, 2016; Larson & Chang, 2016).

FUTURE TRENDS OF AGILE AND DATA ANALYTICS

An effort to create CRISP-DM 2.0 has been abandoned, outlining a need to determine if a more comprehensive and detailed methodology for data analytics is required. Jurney (2017) has proposed the agile data analytics manifesto that outlines seven principles, which include iteration, prototyping, data-driven, process metadata, and determining critical path to results. As outlined, best practices in data analytics are still emerging, and this research has highlighted many of the current trends. Future research will determine if a more comprehensive methodology for data analytics is needed, and the basis for this research will rely data analytics project maturity.

CONCLUSION

Big data brings challenges to traditional data management practices, introduces new and diverse technologies, and drives the need for deeper skillsets to wrangle data. Big data in data analytics coupled with the speed that data analytics is evolving increases project complexity. ASD values and principles can be leveraged to improve data analytics project delivery. Areas of benefit come from improved process flexibility and close collaboration with business stakeholders. Some of the barriers of applying ASD to data analytics projects include the time-box development cycles and the focus on producing high-quality software. Data analytics value lies in producing new insight, thus producing high-quality software become less of a priority. By synthesizing ASD principles, CRISP-DM processes, with known best practices to create the data analytics project delivery framework, this research aligns the use of theory translated into practical application.

REFERENCES

Abbasi, A., & Adjeroh, D. (2014). Social media analytics for smart health. *IEEE Intelligent Systems*, 29(2), 60–64.

Abbasi, A., Suprateek S., & Chiang, R. (2016). Big Data Research in Information Systems: Toward an Inclusive Research Agenda. *Journal of the Association for Information Systems*. 17(2), i.

Alnoukari, M. (2015). *ASD-BI: An Agile Methodology for Effective Integration of Data Mining in Business Intelligence Systems*. Hershey, PA: IGI Publishing.

Aston, B. (2017). 9 Project Management Methodologies Made Simple: The Complete Guide For Project Managers. Retrieved from www.thedigitalprojectmanager.com/project-management-methodologies-made-simple/#agile.

Bole, U., Popovič, A., Žabkar, J., Papa, G., & Jaklič, J. (2015). A case analysis of embryonic data mining success. *International Journal of Information Management*, 352.

Beck, K., *et al.* (2001). The Agile Manifesto for Software Development. www.agilemanifesto.org/.

Davenport, T. H. (2013). Analytics 3.0. *Harvard Business Review*, 91(12), 64–72.

Davenport, T. H. (2014). Big data@work: Dispelling the myths, uncovering the opportunities. *Harvard Business Review Press*, p. 228.

Davenport, T. (2015). 5 Essential Principles for Understanding Analytics. *Harvard Business School Cases*, 1.

Denning, S. (2015). Agile: The World's Most Popular Innovation Engine. Forbes. Retrieved from www.forbes.com/sites/stevedenning/2015/07/23/the-worlds-most-popular-innovation-engine/#7705aaf37c76.

Gartner Research (2015). Gartner Says Business Intelligence and Analytics Leaders Must Focus on Mindsets and Culture to Kick Start Advanced Analytics. Gartner Business Intelligence & Analytics Summit 2015. Retrieved April 10, 2017, from www.gartner.com/newsroom/id/3130017.

Grimes, S., & Intelligent Enterprise (2006). BI Deployments, Methodology Does Matter. San Mateo, 9.

Halper, F. (2015). Next-Generation Analytics and Platforms for Business Success. TDWI Research Report. www.tdwi.org.

Halper, F. (2016). Data analytics and Big Data: Enterprise paths to Success. TDWI Research Report. www.tdwi.org.

Jurney, R. (2017). Agile Data analytics 2.0. O'Reilly Publishing. 1st edition. ISBN-13: 978–1491960110.

Keith, E. R. (2006). Agile Software Development Processes A Different Approach to Software Design. Retrieved from www.cs.nyu.edu/courses/spring03/V22.0474-001/lectures/agile/AgileDevelopmentDifferentApproach.pdf.

Larson, D., & Chang, V. (2016). A review and future direction of agile, business intelligence, analytics and data analytics. *International Journal of Information Management*, 36700–36710. doi: 10.1016/j.ijinfomgt.2016.04.013.

Layton, M., & Ostermiller, S. (2017). *Agile Project Management*, 2nd edition.

Marbán, O., Mariscal, G., & Segovia, J. (2009). A Data Mining & Knowledge Discovery Process Model. In *Data Mining and Knowledge Discovery in Real Life Applications*. Vienna, Austria: I-Tech, pp. 438–453.

Mayer-Schönberger, V. & Cukier, K. *A Revolution That Will Transform How We Live, Work, and Think*. Eamon Dolan/Houghton Mifflin Harcourt, p. 242.

Mena, J. (2011). *Machine Learning Forensics for Law Enforcement, Security, and Intelligence*. Boca Raton, FL: CRC Press (Taylor & Francis Group).

Sahu, A. K. (2016). The Criticism of Data Mining Applications and Methodologies. *International Journal Of Advanced Research In Computer Science*, 7(1), 52–55.

Sim, J. (2014). Consolidation of success factors in data mining projects. *GSTF Journal on Computing (JoC)*, 4(1), 66–73. Retrieved from www.ezproxy.library.nyu.edu:2048/login?url=http://search.proquest.com/docview/1642381546?accountid=12768.

11

Data Analytics and Scrum

Bert Brijs

CONTENTS

INTRODUCTION

Defining metrics and pointing out the necessary data to produce these metrics in the agile world is the very ambitious goal of this chapter. That is because this chapter is probably the most exotic one in this book. It deals with reconciling two totally different worlds, each with their own rules and cultures and yet, it may also be a road map to one of the most valuable endeavors if you can bridge the gap between these two worlds.

This chapter explains the origins and reasons for the gap between data analytics for project management and Scrum, and it develops these problems further in a discussion on the differences between transaction processing and analytical processing application development as these are completely different project types. It concludes with a description of a case in transaction application development and elaborates on the approach to data analytics in projects for "classical" business intelligence.

MIXING OIL AND WATER: DATA ANALYTICS AND SCRUM

The agile culture is human-centered and believes in self-organizing teams. This is far from the "Taylor and Fayol"-like division of work supervised by non participating (project) managers who need a spreadsheet with numbers instead of observing the process during the stand-ups, the retrospectives, and the backlog grooming sessions.

The agile world is about facing the client and responding to his requirements with pragmatism to produce practical solutions delivered rapidly in short cycles of stories that yield a concrete functional aspect of the total solution. Estimating these stories is a joint effort of analysts and developers together with the product owner, and each project has its own ecosystem where the complexity of the development may produce internal consistency, but this will by no means imply conformity with external, objective standards. Using metrics from past projects may provide a rough benchmark for want of a better standard but only if all aspects of the project at hand are equal to the past, which is not very realistic: team compositions, frameworks, analysis quality etc. will vary over time.

In other words, the maturity of the team members, the group dynamics, the intrinsic motivation of key members, the hygienic factors like a nice office space, flexible working hours, and, last but not least, the client and the product owner will greatly influence the productivity of the team.

And then there is that phenomenon called "estimatiophobia": the deeply engrained fear of developers to address the project with an entrepreneurial spirit, that sense of "I don't control every aspect of this project but I have the will to succeed. Therefore I stick my neck out and estimate this work at € *xyz.*"

Instead, developers tend to reduce risk as much as possible, act cautiously when the project manager (PM) asks for commitments of time, quality, cost and all these other tedious metrics that only PMs can be interested in. "Me, I just want to build a perfect solution!"

The result? At best, overestimated efforts and social loafing at worst, outright fraud.

So one thing is already clear: it is hard to find benchmarks for any metric produced in agile projects. Especially when story points (SPs) express the relative complexity within the project, the only usable information data analytics can produce is validated on consistency within that specific project.

If you are tackling large development tracks with more than one Scrum team, the need for normalizing the value of SPs will become evident. The teams will have to put some effort in adjusting their estimates to provide a transversal insight in the project's progress.

If you need a shared basis for project management decisions on scope, budget, quality, and throughput time, you need to normalize the various teams' story point estimates in an orderly way., The scaled agile framework (SAFe) offers you the methodology to do so. There is ample information on the SAFe for more on this.*

The analytics world is about creating one version of the facts, verifying these facts using external sources if available, or reproducing the analysis on new data for validation and exploiting these facts to produce actionable information for decision-makers. In short, a benchmark: all of the stuff that scares the hell out of a Scrum meeting.

Is this the end of this chapter? No, there is hope. Years of involvement in agile projects for software development and for business intelligence projects where analytics have contributed to better project management decisions have produced a few clues. But don't get your hopes too high: these few empirically based methods are under the assumption that further improvement on this body of knowledge is needed. Moreover don't expect fancy statistics, let alone advanced analytics. Most of these known metrics are descriptive stats: burndown of sprints, releases, velocity, and so on.

AGILE AND DATA ANALYTICS IN OLTP AND OLAP

For project managers who have no prior knowledge of application development, here's a primer on online transactional processing (OLTP) and online analytical processing (OLAP).

OLTP applications support business processes like selling and developing customer relationships, shipping and warehousing products, booking incoming and outgoing invoices, and collecting and paying money. It is typical for transaction processing that the database operations support transactions using insert, update, read, and delete operations and the object of each process is one: one client record, one SKU record, etc. Of course, lists are also select queries but within the scope of

---

* www.scaledagileframework.com/iteration-planning/.

the transaction support system: list all clients with an order data before a certain date, find SKUs with a warehouse entry date of last year, etc.

OLAP applications are—in contrast to OLTP—transversal in their approach. That means combining data coming from various business processes to produce meaningful answers to business questions. For example, to answer the question, "Who are my most valuable customers?" you need to get data from the customer relationship system, the production and warehouse management system, and the financial system. With the advent of big data, social media data, and other unstructured data from surveys, call center interactions and reviews will add to the complexity of an OLAP application.

For more on these two worlds, read the works of Ralph Kimball, Bill Inmon, and Dan Linstedt as the champions of OLAP and Philip Bernstein for OLTP.

Agile software development has been around for a while. Developing OLTP applications is fundamentally different from developing OLAP applications. In the OLTP world, there is clear link between the requirements, the use cases and the user stories and finally, the deliverables.

Let's use a hotel application as a case in point.

The requirements are unequivocal: the client needs support for well-defined business processes:

- Managing the rooms and their amenities
- Managing the cleaning and catering
- Managing loyal clients and visitors
- Managing bookings, check ins and check outs

Each business process leads to clear use cases, constraints, and requirements that are relatively easy to convert into user stories, which are in turn easy to estimate for complexity. The planning poker can be played with all partners engaged on equal foot in the process. The client and the product owner know what they want and the developers and analysts know how to deliver the goods.

The OLAP world is something completely different. The links are a lot vaguer as the following two examples will illustrate. Let's start with an agile data mining project where project data analytics makes no sense at all and finish with a typical business intelligence project where reports are the concrete deliverables.

An agile data mining project to develop a recommender system for libraries has the following processes in scope:

Library members allow us to use their data for analyzing lending history data to find links between books, music, and films that may be useful to produce recommender algorithms. The historical data of all consenting members are used to build, exploit, and test recommender models. External data sources need to be examined for their contribution to the recommender models. The models are internally validated and the best model is chosen and rolled out to a sample of the member community for real-life validation.

The recommender model is tweaked further and rolled out to the entire community.

This is closer to an R&D project than to a development track and the metrics produced are, at best, indicators of velocity, the most basic analytics an agile project can produce. There are simply no metrics with any predictive value available in such a project. Project managers who want to keep the scope and the cost under control may want to work with very strict time boxing, tweaking the epics to stay within the boundaries. But this is not without risk as datamining projects need to backtrack to the first project steps at any moment. In other words, the definition of "done" may alter a few times during the project. The reason is simple: rearranging the data, tweaking the model, and creating variations on the analytical algorithms may increase or decrease the information value of the analytics.

The second example from the OLAP world has more useful project data, ready for analysis. An end-to-end business intelligence (BI) project may provide more handles to the project manager for analytical support. That is because many BI projects are wrongfully translated into application development projects for reports:*

Each report requirement description should include the following descriptives:

- What are the measures and by which dimension should they be presented. For example, I want a volume report per product line per customer per year to date, year minus one and year minus two.
- Refine the previous expression by adding the granularity and the drill down possibilities: e.g. With "customer" I mean every individual VAT number, not the department who ordered the product. The time drill down stops at a weekly level.

---

* Bert Brijs, *Business Analysis for Business Intelligence*, CRC Books, Boca Raton, FL, 2013, pp. 307–308.

- Description of derived or "static" attributes, which may not be present in the foreseen data warehouse solution: e.g. totals per week per account manager or store type, parking lot surface
- Users of the report
- Presentation options (screen, pdf document, spreadsheet, executable)
- A lay out example if necessary. This feature depends on the degrees of freedom the front-end tool offers its users.
- Business rules, which may affect the comments, the presentation, or other user aspects of the reports: e.g. "a customer is a party that has bought at least one product within 12 months."

Instead of exploiting all decision support opportunities the available data may provide, the client has a clear view on the scope of the project defining dimensions and metrics in simple stories like:

"As a finance manager I want to have a daily report of the credit risk per customer."

Or "as a logistics manager I want to simulate various demand scenarios on my inventory positions."

Yet, the best performing BI projects need a thorough insight into the data and application landscape to produce meaningful stories:*

In complex environments, an application landscape can provide a high level lineage view on crucial data like customers and employees. For example: an organization may have different input possibilities like a checkout, a call center, and external customer data sources which need to be reconciled in a customer master data repository.

In this phase, a first estimate of data volumes may be useful to determine the technical scope of the project.

In case of heavy security demands (e.g. HRM analytics or BI for legal or policing purposes) the metadata should also include which profiles (or even persons) have access rights to which data.

Finally, a conceptual and/or logical data model of the data warehouse or the data mart is both the result and the documentation of the business analysis process.

This should provide enough input for the project definition and the project charter.

You will put forward that this may be counterintuitive to the agile manifesto, but isn't pragmatism at the very heart of this manifesto? Once the data landscape hurdle has been taken, the agile approach is ready to

---

* Ibid. pp. 260–262.

deliver bits and pieces of functionality. Omitting this step may lead to the same root cause as in the aforementioned data mining project: changing definitions of "done."

But are all parties on an equal foot in this poker process? You may experience this is not the case for the following reasons. First, there can be a long journey between the raw data and their conversion into meaningful results. This goes beyond estimating the join between tables or creating views and all the usual stuff that is required for operational reporting on a single application. BI, by definition is about integrating multiple sources, each with their specific perspective on reality. The business analyst and the BI designer have the advantage over the client and the product owner. They will have more insight in the complexity of access, and loading and transformation of the data into actionable information. And then there's the data quality issue: what level of data quality is sufficient to conclude the sprints as "Done"? Won't this lead to new iterations afterwards and if so, are these parts of the project or do we allocate them to a new project? Again, the analyst and the designer are more in control than the product owner. But let's assume all this does not pose a problem to the 'weaker' party. In that case, there are ways and means to mix the analytics oil with the agile water.

AN OLTP CASE: THE HOTEL APPLICATION

Let's get our hands dirty and assemble the base data about the team, the story points (SPs), and the metrics used.

The Scrum team is assembled as shown in Tables 11.1 and 11.2.

The SPs are budgeted in advance as follows: The cost increases at a faster rate than the throughput time as increasing complexity requires "heavier," more expensive profiles. At the outset of the project the technical team illustrates what exactly these story point levels mean in practice (Table 11.3). At the outset of the project, the team commits to keeping the estimates as low as possible, which implies keeping the grain of each story as small as possible. Of course, basic setups, usually done in Sprint 0 can be benchmarked against other projects, e.g. installing a virtual machine, creating dev, test, UAT, and prod environments with their respective databases, libraries, and frameworks. But let's leave this out of the scope of this exercise.

TABLE 11.1

Composition of the Scrum Team for an OLTP Application

Name	Function	Level	Availability
Tom Hollow	.NET architect	Senior	10%
Tommy Willow	Front End Developer	Senior	60%
Max Sverdlov	Front End Developer	Junior	80%
Bart De Lanoye	Back End	Senior	30%
Chelsea Nieberding	User interface developer	Junior	90%
Bart Brice	Analyst	Senior	50%
Ludo Abicht	Project Manager	Medior	50%

TABLE 11.2

Budgeted Cost per Level of Complexity

SP	Estimated Throughput Time	Cost Estimate	Cost/ SP
1	4 hours	€ 200,—	€ 200,—
2	12 hours	€ 700,—	€ 350,—
3	20 hours	€ 1,200,—	€ 400,—
5	32 hours	€ 2,080,—	€416,—
8	56 hours	€ 3,920,—	€490,—
13	Not accepted	N/A	N/A

TABLE 11.3

Translation of Story Complexity into Business Requirements for OLTP

SP	Technical Description	Example for the Business Analyst
1	Creating a table with a few fields without complex validations	Registration data for a client
2	A form with dropdown fields, simple validation, cascading updates and deletes	Booking a stay in the hotel
3	Setting up communication flow with notifications, triggers,…	Handling the reservation communications with the customers
5	Calculation engine	An engine to calculate optimum pricing as a function of availability and customer demand
8	Setting up fine-grained security	Making customer data access GDPR compliant

The project setup is as follows:

- Create the backlog of user stories and epics.
- Group the stories in sprints based on technical aspects.
- Groom the stories with the team to check for consistency.
- Estimate the stories per sprint.
- Develop the stories and report the following phases:
  - Accepted stories
  - In progress
  - Code review
  - Functional test
  - Rework
  - Done

As soon as Sprint 1 was under way, the measures of throughput time and cost were logged from the timesheets and the KANBAN board:

Project
    Id Story
Complexity
- Stage 1: Acceptation—Tech team
- Stage 2: 1st time—In Progress
- Stage 3: 1st time—Code reviewed
- Stage 4: 1st time to Functional Test
- Stage 5: Date done
- Stage 6: Story points delivered
- Stage 7: Story points accepted by the client
Remarks

A set of lagging and leading metrics will help the self-organizing team to adjust for better performance.

Lagging Indicators and Metrics

This list of descriptive statistics goes from global to more specific measures. In most cases it is a simple count of SPs in a specified context or filter:

- Number of SPs completed: the velocity of done stories.
- Stories started but not done: number of story points in progress.

- Discovered work during the sprint: SPs added to the sprint and to the backlog.
- Accepted velocity: the SPs that were done and accepted by the product owner during the sprint.
- Some other events counted:
- Impediments discovered, resolved, and remaining
- Scope increase or decrease during the sprint
- Budgeted vs. actual cost of the total project

Leading Indicators and Metrics

Sprint pass predictions: after a few iterations we can collect sufficient data to predict the number of stories (i.e. story points) that will be included within the next sprint. This in itself is a good indicator for short-term predictions like intermediate delivery of functionality or of epics.

This metric is basically observation of the team's behavior. For example, in Sprint 1 the team included 60 SPs and finished 50 or 83% of them. Sprint 2 was composed of 55 SPs and completed 48 or 87% and so on. The team agrees on an estimate between 48 and 52 SPs in Sprint 4and the following sprints as the median estimate was 50.

With an initial backlog of an estimated 550 SPs we can make a first and very rough prediction of total throughput time: about 11 times two weeks or 22 weeks on the premise of equal availability and capacity, the 12th Sprint is planned for contingency. In the next few metrics we will further refine that number.

Capacity prediction for the next sprint: here, the team members who are not 100% allocated to the project block their agendas for work on the sprint and count the available person days. This figure should be kept as constant as possible and in the opposite case, produce a red flag for the planning sessions. Table 11.4 shows these metrics in one overview.

Table 11.5 with the timesheet data is used for showing deviations from the estimated cost per story.

Take your time: you will need at least four or five sprints completed before you can trust the data. The budgeted cost per story is compared to the actual cost. From this comparison only one lesson needs to be learned: is the team improving its estimation accuracy over time and do we as a team look for the root causes of the variances?

TABLE 11.4

Scrum Data: Lagging and Leading Indicators

Item	# SPs	Completed	Started	Discovered	Accepted	Impediments Discovered	Impediments Resolved	Impediments Remaining	Scope Increase	Scope Decrease	Total Budgeted Cost	Total Actual Cost	Cost Delta	Sprint Pass Predictions	Capacity Prediction Person/Days	Total Throughput Estimate In Weeks
Unit of Measure	SP	SP	SP	SP	SP	SP	SP	SP	SP	SP	€	€	€	SP	Days	Weeks
Initial Backlog	550										192.440				35	18
Sprint 1	60	50	58	0	48	1	1	0	0	0	192.440	196.180	3.740	55	35	22
Backlog	490	500	492	492	502				502	502						
Sprints	55	48	55	2	53	0	0	0	2		196.180	194.710	2.270		36	22
Backlog	447	454	447	500	449				451	451						
Sprint 3	50	48	50	0	49	2	0	2	0	0	194.710	191.690	−750		32	24
Backlog	401	403	401	451	402				402	402						
Sprint 4	50														32	
Sprints	50														32	
Sprint 8	50															
Sprint 7	50															
Sprints	50															
Sprint 9 (baseline)	50															
Sprint 10	50															
Sprint 11 (1st Adjustment}	50															
Sprint 12 (2nd Adjustment)	1															

TABLE 11.5

Comparing Budgeted vs Actual Work per Story

Date	Team Member	Time in Decimal Hours	Rate in €	Story_ID	SP	Activity	Cost	Cumulative Cost per Story	Benchmark
02/14/17	Tom Hollow	2	90	1	3	.NET Architect	180	180	1,200
02/15/17	Tommy Willow	2	90	1	3	Front End Development	180	360	1,200
02/16/17	Bart De Lanoye	4	90	1	3	Back End Development	360	720	1,200
02/16/17	Max Sverdlov	4	50	1	3	Front End Development	200	920	1,200
02/16/17	Tommy Willow	1	90	1	3	Code Review	90	1,010	1,200
02/17/17	Chelsea Nieberding	2	50	1	3	User Interface Jobs	100	**1,110**	**1,200**
02/14/17	Tom Hollow	3	90	2	2	Front End Development	270	270	700
02/15/17	Max Sverdlov	4	50	2	2	Front End Development	200	470	700
02/16/17	Max Sverdlov	8	50	2	2	Front End Development	400	870	700
02/16/17	Chelsea Nieberding	8	50	2	2	User Interface Jobs	400	1,270	700
02/16/17	Tommy Willow	0.5	90	2	2	Code Review	45	1,315	700
02/17/17	Chelsea Nieberding	6	50	2	2	User Interface Jobs	300	**1,615**	**700**
02/20/17	Tom Hollow	6	90	3	5	.NET Architect	540	540	2,080

(Continued)

TABLE 11.5 (Continued)

Comparing Budgeted vs Actual Work per Story

Date	Team Member	Time in Decimal Hours	Rate in €	Story_ID	SP	Activity	Cost	Cumulative Cost per Story	Benchmark
02/20/17	Tommy Willow	2	90	3	5	Front End Development	180	720	2,080
02/20/17	Max Sverdlov	6	50	3	5	Front End Development	300	1,020	2,080
02/20/17	Bart De Lanoye	8	90	3	5	Back End Development	720	1,740	2,080
02/20/17	Chelsea Nieberding	2	50	3	5	User Interface Jobs	100	1,840	2,080
02/20/17	Bart Brice	8	90	3	5	Analysis	720	2,560	2,080
02/20/17	Ludo Abicht	3	70	3	5	Project Management	210	2,770	2,080
02/20/17	Tommy Willow	2	90	3	5	Code Review	180	2,950	2,080
02/21/17	Max Sverdlov	4	50	4	2	Front End Development	200	200	700
02/21/17	Chelsea Nieberding	2	50	4	2	User Interface Jobs	100	300	700
02/21/17	Bart Brice	1	90	4	2	Analysis	90	390	700
02/21/17	Ludo Abicht	1	70	4	2	Project Management	70	460	700
02/22/17	Chelsea Nieberding	1.5	50	4	2	User Interface Jobs	75	535	700
02/22/17	Max Sverdlov	2	50	4	2	Front End Development	100	635	700
02/22/17	Bart Brice	0.5	90	4	2	Analysis	45	680	700

Since cost, activities, and duration are transparent the team can decide on improving the mix of effort per story. In other words, the team starts asking questions like:

- "Do we need time for code review if a senior developer is working in tandem with a junior developer?"
- "What part of the development could be allocated to the further development of the framework instead of charging the project with the cost?"
- "Which types of stories are mostly under—or overestimated?"
- "Is the analyst providing sufficient input for a correct estimate?"

After the first sprint, this analysis can also inspire the team to improve capacity planning by comparing the daily burn rate with the available capacity (Table 11.6). Apparently only the dates 16 and 20 February showed optimum use of available capacity.

The team will need to come up with answers to the five "why" questions starting with questions like:

- Why wasn't the team fully allocated to the sprint?
- Why were there technical impediments?
- Why wasn't there contingency for blocking issues?

The team can also learn from its success: story no. 1, 9, 11, 13, and 14 were considerably more cost effective than estimated. Again, a "five why" analysis may bring some new ideas to the group's performance. In other words, even if the analytics stay within the group, try to avoid negative feedback loops; look for positive cause-and-effect chains and the team's performance will improve as a result.

SCRUM, DATA ANALYTICS, AND OLAP

As previously stated, this is not a match made in heaven: working in small iterations in data warehousing can only start once the foundations for these iterations are laid. And that is the only workable way to obtain meaningful results.

TABLE 11.6

Analyzing the Sprint Results

Story Points/Story	3	2	5	2	2	3	2	5	3	2	5	2	3	8	
							Story ID								Burn Rate/
Date	1	2	3	4	5	6	7	8	9	10	11	12	13	14	Day
2/14/17	180	360					90	90					90	720	1,530
2/15/17	180	100					180	400						630	1,490
2/16/17	550	560					410	590						1,110	3,220
2/17/17	100	300						290						450	1,140
2/20/17			2,310					890	380						3,580
2/21/17				460					410		45				915
2/22/17				220							595				815
2/23/17					885					345	485				1,715
2/24/17						1,080				345			90		1,515
2/28/17												850	810		1,660
Cost per Story	1,010	1,320	2,310	680	885	1,080	680	2,260	790	690	1,125	850	990	2,910	17,580
Cost per SP	337	660	462	340	443	360	340	452	263	345	225	425	330	364	Total To Date
SP Estimate	400	350	416	350	350	400	350	416	400	350	416	350	400	490	

So here's the deal: just like we accept a Sprint Zero for setting up the technical environment, why don't we introduce the Sprint Minus One to set up the correct data model by analyzing the total analytical potential of the data sources even when their potential is far beyond the initial analytical requirements?

Sprint Minus One and Architecture

The analysts' task is in essence charting the known and potentially unknown analytical requirements, translate these into data requirements, identifying the sources and their feasibility for extracting, transforming, and loading the data. It includes identifying potential data quality risks, opportunities for reference and master data initiatives and translating this into a comprehensive target model using dimensions and fact tables. Please give preference to a star schema as the ultimate target model as this is close to the users' world view and because most analytical front-end tools benefit from the technical performance of this data model. It depends on the existing knowledge, the strategic options, and the volatility of the analytical requirements if there is a need for an intermediate storage in the third normal form (3NF), a data vault or even an anchor model (6NF). If that is the case and updates to an existing model or the creation of an entirely new model is needed, this sprint may take a few months and one may ask the question whether this activity should be allocated to the project as the analogy with framework development in the OLTP case is obvious. Some financial managers will use the old rule of thumb of "crossing the boundary" and allocate the cost and effort entirely to the project. Experience from a large retail client who applied this rule proved them wrong. The retailer allocated information infrastructure costs that were in essence transversal and beneficial to all departments and subsidiaries to the project that put it in the requirements. Needless to say that many projects were either killed or reduced in scope. The outcome of the reduced projects was dramatic. Every business sponsor avoided this step and every project was defined as an end-to-end source–target-report endeavor, leading to erratic results like six-time ("time" not "calendar"!) dimensions in an enterprise data warehouse with 1,500 tables. It also led to over 20,000 reports, which—after thorough analysis—could be reduced to less than 5,000. And you can add to that opportunity cost the endless discussions over which version of the facts was needed for which report, nor the frustrations of the back-room developers to do the actual extract–load–transform tasks of all these silo projects in an orderly way.

Creating a match between agile and OLAP is no trivial exercise as the following article on the BA4BI blog from May 2013 illustrates.*

In this blog "Business Analysis for Business Intelligence," seven principles guiding business intelligence enterprise architecture are summed up. These are the contents of the article:

1. Focus on people, not technology.
2. Perfection is the enemy of the good.
3. Iterative and incremental.
4. Build it first, then talk about it.
5. See the entire picture but use small increments.
6. Make it attractive: user-centric and practical, no academic geek gymnastics.
7. These are the deliverables:

   Customer support for the enterprise architecture
   A vision and plan to achieve that vision
   A collection of models and documentation describing the architecture

So here's the take away: don't ever allocate data infrastructure improvements to a single project. It's about enterprise architecture. End of discussion.

As soon as Sprint Zero Minus One and Sprint Zero are finished, the analysts should have a backlog of stories ready.

Managing the granularity of these stories is no trivial task as it can be hard not to overdo on stories of five, eight, or even thirteen story points.

A few tips:

- Work table per table: in a complex environment the target table may take the lead. For example, if your customer dimension needs to integrate multiple sources, create an epic, and work out stories source per source table.
- Separate the metadata analysis from the data requirements analysis in separate epics.
- Define separate sprints for end-to-end testing.
- Split report requirements into header–footer and report body sprints.

---

* http://bit.ly/AgileEnterpriseArchitecture (published on 21 May 2013).

TABLE 11.7

Translation of Story Complexity into Business Requirements for OLAP

SP	Technical Description	Example for the Business Analyst
1	Creating a static dimension table Defining and creating a simple extract	A time dimension Extracting data with simple transformations like CAST
2	Creating a simple dynamic dimension table Unit testing	A ship to dimension Testing one ETL sequence
3	Creating a complex dimension table	A customer dimension
5	Loading dynamic dimension tables	A customer dimension
8	Loading a simple fact table	A factless fact table describing events
13	Loading a complex fact table Implementing a change data capture rule	Sales fact with many dimensions Incremental load of changing dimensions and facts
21	Doing a historical load	The sales from the last 3 years

Once you have a grip on the stories, comparable to an OLTP project, the world's your oyster!

Table 11.7 shows an example of story point levels in an OLAP project. As you notice, higher order stories are simply unavoidable. The tensions between agile and OLAP will always remain.

EPILOGUE

If product owners accept the restrictions on data analytics in an agile environment and accept the reality that Scrum teams are self-organizing teams then they can position their job in an optimum way.

What this means for your job as a product owner:

- At best, you're the coach, not the leader; most of the time you're a facilitator.
- Work with short feedback loops.
- For any data provided to you by the team, return meaningful information and do it fast.

- Planning is at its worst *outside* the team, usually *with* the team, and ideally *within* the team.
- Knowledge sharing is of vital importance when you put a diversity of specialists in a team. Your job is to facilitate this.
- Make sure you and the team accept the story behind the data by looking for the root causes thereby avoiding the "blame game."

Index

Note: Page numbers followed by *f* indicate figures; those followed by *t* indicate tables.

Printed in the United States
by Baker & Taylor Publisher Services